Cats work like *this*

David St John Thomas was a British publisher who founded David & Charles in the UK and USA, and *Writers News Magazine*. David wrote over 30 books including *For the Love of a Cat*.

David's son, Gareth St John Thomas, is the founder and CEO of Exisle Publishing, based in Australia and New Zealand. He has been involved in the book industry since he was eleven years old, when he started helping his dad at David & Charles. Now, his mission with Exisle is to bring books into the world from voices that otherwise wouldn't have been heard, and to give readers something with heart. Gareth has written other adult and children's books including *Finding True Connections* and *Grandpa's Noises*.

Cats work like *this*

David St John Thomas & Gareth St John Thomas

EXISLE
PUBLISHING

First published 2022

Exisle Publishing Pty Ltd
PO Box 864, Chatswood, NSW 2057, Australia
226 High Street, Dunedin, 9016, New Zealand
www.exislepublishing.com

A CiP record for this book is available from the National Library of Australia.
ISBN 978-1-925820-75-1
Designed by Mark Thacker
Typeset in Warnock Pro regular 11 on 17.5pt
Printed in China

This book uses paper sourced under ISO 14001 guidelines from well-
managed forests and other controlled sources.

10 9 8 7 6 5 4 3 2 1

Dedicated to Nathan

Contents

Introduction

My father David St John Thomas was a driven man. He was a journalist, a market gardener, a publisher, writer, businessman, train expert and an enthusiast for much of life. He wrote nearly 30 of his own books and oversaw the publishing of thousands of others. Life was generally good; he enjoyed his work and was normally healthy. Of course, everything wasn't perfect — three wives (though only the last one attended his funeral) attest a little to that, and he died no older than his father at 83.

David never followed any trends or styles or fashions. For example, he always preferred small rural places to live and made friends with whom he could and wanted to. Most of all he loved travelling by train and ship. Many of his friends were cats, who often sought him out when his routine walks crossed their territories. He had a soothing voice for them and in turn a chat with a cat seemed to take his stress away. He knew cats are creatures of habit so if a cat wasn't already in its normal spot Dad would, often successfully, wait a few minutes for his friend to arrive to resume yesterday's conversation.

After he died, I was working through David's papers (he wrote to the very end) and discovered that the beginning of this book, *Cats Work Like This*, already had its concept and the first chapter. So with David over my shoulder I have set out to finish it, and as well as discovering something more about cats and, with apologies to T.S. Eliot, we may get to sense more of David's terpsichorean powers. With his father, the poet Gilbert Thomas, David had written a book about their huge model railway, *Double Headed*. So, in a way I am building upon a tradition.

The following first chapter has the last words David wrote for publication when he was beginning to be overrun by ill health.

1

Cats work like *this*

The title of this book is provocative, for the very idea of cats working to a prescribed routine is somewhat facile.

Above all, cats are individualists, following no rules or prescriptions. Yet they do have their own natural ways of procedure. 'This is the way cats proceed' might have been a more accurate approach but with cats any generalisations are dangerous.

There are indeed few things about cats that are predictable ... other than that they will surprise you. For weeks they might settle on a favourite couch, but as soon as you expect that to happen, they will find a new favourite resting place.

Something I always enjoy is watching them size things up. My male cat has been doing this for years. When he visits his favourite room of the moment, he carefully looks around taking everything in; he carefully considers where he might be most comfortable on this occasion. Typically cat-like, he might jump up to his favourite resting place for weeks at a time, but then suddenly abandon it for somewhere different. The only predictable thing is that he places great store on his choice of location … and that having chosen it for weeks he will suddenly make a change. Comfort is everything, even if it takes time to decide where luxuriating comfort best exists or has been moved to.

Occasionally, he enjoys being set down on his current favourite surface, but a few days later promptly jumps off it as though it were the least acceptable place in the whole wide world and why did I have to interfere.

He and his sister often choose to be together and will spend the first quarter of an hour grooming each other. But should we be foolish enough to put them side by side, they jump off as though we have made the silliest of mistakes. So, I suppose that in cat terms we have. Cats must select their own comfort and friendships with what disdain they treat what we've done. Even though it was thoroughly acceptable the last couple of nights or even weeks. 'Not that place again,' they seem to say as they jump off.

But then, while for weeks at a time one of them jumps into my lap for a cuddle, suddenly one night they cannot bear to feel my touch. In a previous book I told the story of how a literary agent, who had temporarily left me in her lounge while she concluded business with another customer, was annoyed to find me with both her cats on my lap. 'They never do that. You must be weird to attract them but then I've never understood you or your publishing list.' My secret was to allow the cats to make their own choices. So often cats shy away from excitable people, especially young women whose laps they might ultimately have chosen if left to make their own move. It's not so much that cats are unpredictable as that they like to make their own move and choice.

I love exchanging greetings with unknown cats on a walk, but always allow them to make the first move, perhaps having spoken to them and stooped down so that I am not an overpowering presence. Always let the feline make the first move.

Though there are many more cats than dogs, the human understanding of them is often painfully woeful.

Cats versus dogs

While dogs must be licensed cats generally lack independent legal status. If your dog steals from a neighbour, it is your liability to make amends. The case could indeed go to court. But the law generally ignores cats, which, among other things, means we don't know how many there are of them. Almost certainly, cats outnumber dogs and make a greater impact on society, many children's first pet being a cat (or more likely a playful kitten). Their influence on society and the quotes and comments and sayings about them are greater than for dogs.

But think of the problems if they did have legal status, such as their deciding to move in next door where life seems to offer greater comfort. Cats are above the law and seem to know it as they exercise their freedom to move home or to steal someone's Sunday dinner.

While dogs have been bred to be man's best friend (i.e. obedient servant), cats need staff to serve their needs. Dogs and cat lovers tend to be very different. You of course don't have to dislike dogs to be a cat lover but just recognize the difference and know when you must serve instead of being served.

What I enjoy about cats is knowing they will only accept my friendship when recognizing it is genuinely given. Especially with the appropriate emphasis given to them, my cats have learnt the meaning of many words. Typically, though setting their own agenda, they want to please and usually avoid doing things they know we dislike. Purring on a comfortable lap is more pleasurable than being shouted at. When they are defiantly disobedient their ears flatten, as they fear they will be shouted at. They prospect for a comfortable lap and quickly take the hint when I tap my lap as a kind of invitation.

Cats know when to turn the charm on and are masterly at getting their way. When a friend came to stay and one evening sat in their favourite chair, she was soon so stared at as to feel uncomfortable. She moved and, mission accomplished, the cats regained 'their' territory. Cats have many ways of making us know we're not doing the right thing by their standards. Except possibly when it comes to food, they share a keen sense of what is right and what upsets routine. Ours have been trained never to expect food from our plates and even trained to not jump on the table when it's not laid. Partly, their behaviour is based on not upsetting us and avoiding being shouted at. They no doubt think of our rules as a means of keeping our pride up but there's a *modus vivendi* between the species.

Cats and children

Many children's first pet is a kitten. There may be no legal transaction, but bundles of emotion are involved, often remembered from childhood into old age.

Do you recall the moment you discovered that your pet cat was a killing machine and delighted in teasing a mouse before making a meal of it? How cruel life could be. The whereabouts and circumstances of where I first saw a cat tease a mouse have long been forgotten in the passage of time, but the horrified emotion is as sharp today as all those dozens of years ago. In fact, the precise point in Hythe Kent, where many childhood holidays were spent, came back to me the night after I had said cats are everywhere — even what was then known as Battersea Dogs Home had a cat in

the director's office. I've even met a cat in a New York publisher's office where a combination of hot drink, background music and feline company was meant to put overseas visitors (potentially interested in acquiring overseas rights) at ease.

In my earlier book, *For the Love of a Cat*, I describe how Sarah, my female cat with great personality, co-operated to make visiting American customers welcome and take the right decisions. If they were volubly opposed to me, she wouldn't be above biting their legs. She was so ultra-loyal to me that if I had a mock fight with my daughter her legs would also be bitten.

Characters

It could be said this applies to every cat, for few cats are not characters in one way or another. But here I have given room to some cats and incidents that especially made their mark on me.

At a market garden where I was temporarily working there was a formally installed regular cat, a busy mouser who many customers had got to know. She cheerfully accepted all the fuss they made of her. To encourage her to supplement her diet with mice and the occasional rat she was given a meagre allowance by the owner. One day a stray walked in and was given a surprisingly warm welcome by the resident cat. Especially surprising was seeing her hold back on eating her own meal just put down and encouraging the stray to share it. Indeed, it was more than that. The resident held off eating any of her food until she had encouraged the stray to share it. I have noticed other examples where cats are not friendly to others yet happily share a meal together.

I love my present cats, brother and sister Arran and Skye, but never had a closer relationship than the first cat of my adult life, Sarah, a Siamese Seal Point who lived into her 21st year. I recall collecting her by myself and her yowling in the car on the way home unless I held one of her tiny paws through the wire of her carrying cage. When we arrived home, she was adamant she wanted to stay on me, although she was only a speck on my 6-foot plus body. When I coughed, she jumped into the air hissing at me, but seemed to understand my 'sorry'. Indeed, she so loved being apologised to that at times I felt she deliberately

put me in the wrong to tack on the apology.

There was a unique bond between us. I'd speak to her on the phone, such as when in Australia on world sales trips. When I returned, she might slink away to register her protest at my absence. But then emotions overcame her, and she would fly into my arms to make up.

Sarah seemed so irreplaceable that for years after she died I went without another cat. Then we found a pair of brother and sister Balinese. They were great characters. Skye, the female with piercing eyes always gazing at one, with whom I have a special bond; and Arran, who loves everyone and jumps to attention when the doorbell rings. They give excellent value in amusing and relaxing us. A cat is a cat as a human is a human, but cats are as deeply varied in the basics of life.

2

Introducing
Mr Ponk

Mr Ponk

Having just transcribed my father's writing above, I am being stared at by Mr Ponk. Cats can look at you, eyes half open or glazed over, or sometimes in a relaxed loving way, other times good-naturedly laughing or blinking at you or, as is the case now, with a very clear 'I am telling you something' stare. This is more than watching over me; you will know that loving cat look, perhaps with an upwards tail. But this is not it, nor is it the serious stare which can be about control or even bordering on anger. If I were a cat this stare is a challenge, but this is none of the above. So, what is he telling me?

Cats are very happy to share information with you. It's often not very complicated. But you need to know the cat, and possibly a few others before you can always be sure of what you are being told. Some cats make humans their primary business. This is more usual for those that are confined indoors but it's not uncommon to meet a feline character managing several households.

Ponk, as he well knows, is a prince. He has at least four households under his control. The rather presumptuous family which claims to 'own' him, caring though their children are, provide his 'home'. So they claim. Mr Ponk might think that the man who lives in the nearby cottage with the wood stove on every day of the year provides a better home. But I suspect the food there is not as good as the pricey little tins I provide (he insists upon by shaking his leg disdainfully at anything else I buy him).

But I am not still and settled enough for Ponk's perfect comfort.

Ponk by the window

My other neighbours, parents of his 'owners' are calmer and have altogether more comfortable furniture so Mr Ponk spends more time there. I imagine that a perfect day for Mr Ponk involves awakening next to the stove, being fed soon after at mine, then playing with the children at his official home, and later a sleep at their grandparents' house and waking up for a good long look out of the window.

The only thing I know about this, of course, is that my guesses will be wrong, but it might explain why Mr Ponk sleeps a lot — his is a busy and complex schedule and that's just dealing with the humans, let alone all the other creatures he must manage. Many cats sleep up to sixteen hours a day, and some more. They always have much to do and also need to have the explosive super energy required for that lightening burst of speed — towards a mouse, away from a dog, across a road or just up that tree because they can.

One of Mr Ponk's more defining attributes is an unfailing courtesy to all visitors. In whichever of his houses he happens to be, everyone is greeted in turn. New friends discovered, old smells remembered, and all prospects for food, attention and trouble fully assessed. Whenever a cat enters a new room you will see that they take a full inventory of what's there. That includes the thousands of unique smells that they sense but humans cannot. In the same way, Mr Ponk takes a full inventory of the smells, styles and mannerisms of every human visitor and you can see that questions are being asked.

Is that towering man with a walking stick safe?
Did that loud woman with chlorine-smelling hair and
a coat that smells of an unknown wet dog leave the
animal in her car? Does that little man in a perfumed
cravat who is ignoring me being respectful and giving
me some space, or maybe he doesn't like cats? Let's go
and sit on him to find out. Ah yes, he does like cats but,
like other men his age, he pretends not to.

Oh, of course the look Mr Ponk is still giving me just says 'feed me now' without his having to resort to any undignified fuss like brushing against legs, gazing at his empty plate in the kitchen or even having to meow his concerns.

Most streets, suburbs and lanes will have a friendly cat or two. Yes, they could well be interested in you and, like Ponk, replete with happy experiences of other humans. Yet, to make friends you will need to be patient and careful about your assumptions.

Walking down a dark inner-city laneway coming home from the train, I first came across a fluffy black-and-white cat who seemed to want to talk. I crouched down and held my hand out. She came up and yowled at me, sniffed my hand and then walked sedately away. That was enough information for that night.

Ponk on a tree stump

The next evening, she was quite voluble and seemed to be telling me about her neighbourhood and the many other cats that were around there. I happened to have some cat treats and let one slip. The cat took it with a shrug that said, 'That's not really what I am about but if you must, thanks,' and then slipped off.

Two nights later I was at the same place. She saw me but ignored me. She was surrounded by other cats and was either too busy or didn't want me to know them as well. The next night I caught a later train and was again ignored. But the following two nights I came back at my normal time and the cat came up for a brief chat. We became friends.

If you want to make friends with your local cats you need to be like them, following a routine and being a little cautious. Of course, a token of esteem does not go amiss at the right time, but don't assume that every cat you meet will look upon you just as a meal ticket. Cats like company and a big friend like you could also come in useful one day. So take your time and be consistent and never ever ignore her.

3

Knowing the territory

For a predator with strong fight and flight aptitudes, knowing their territory is essential. This applies to all things physical and what's going on in your and other house residents' minds.

In the physical realm small changes can make a big difference. A book placed on the floor between two chairs can impede an escape route from the dog or an overly zealous child. A small piece of rubbish in front of a garden or a tree could be hiding prey or possibly obscuring the view of a predator. A towel left on the bathroom stool might offer a new safe place to sleep. A glass of red wine on the white carpeted floor can lead to a lot of attention. Any change anywhere in a cat's territory is something that they will know about. There could be new things to play with, and on a lucky day something unexpected to eat. Some cat people leave small portions of dry food in different places in the house to encourage their cats to get up and explore. This makes the home a more exciting and fulfilling place for housebound cats.

One of a cat's key habits is running a constant set of patrols, indoors and where possible outdoors, to see what has changed. As well as objects moving and arriving, other cats could be intruding into their territory so there is routine sniffing and spraying to be done as well.

If you watch regularly, carefully and unobserved, you will see that cats change the direction of their patrols so everywhere is regularly approached from different angles. Be careful that you are not seen too soon — even though a cat's eyes are just in front of them they will very soon sense you looking at them. Then while pretending not to notice you they will probably start doing something different. A cat's patrol is private business and a clumsy bi-ped could never understand — so while you are watching it's probably more fun for them to try and dig up a favourite plant or two of yours instead.

For a cat, of course, there is much to take in in any sized territory. Imagine if you explored most of your entire known world every day — and if you did, how much more you would know about it and just how demanding a task that would be. There could be some further complexities involved if the cat shares part of the territory and you may find that your cat just visits certain areas at specific times of day as access rights have been divided and defined by inter-feline timeshare agreements.

In my childhood home, Sarah's territory included of course the whole house, which she considered a place for her to be entertained, made a fuss of, kept warm and, when tired, quietly and gently admired. All of this was expected by the occupant of every room, where the quality of the experience was always different. My sister's bedroom, for example, provided stimulating geographical challenges with enormous piles of clothing, bedding, cushions and pillows, and curious but generally inedible things growing out of long-parked coffee mugs.

Watch your cat when it next walks into the room; you might think it's a small space, but for a cat it will be fifteen times bigger than it is for you. There will be hundreds more smells than you know about and much more noise. Caution may be called for. If the cat is familiar with the room, she will have already laid out in her mind where the known risk areas are, such as the dog's normal place or where the tail-grabbing toddler is likely to have crawled to. Pre-armed, the cat walks in already alert and knowing where the in-room safe places are and the best routes to them, plus of course which are the desirable and fun spots. A lot of information is very quickly assessed. If there are no new risks and the known ones manageable, she will normally go to a regular safe base to see in detail what's new. Only when that is fully analyzed will she go to a more entertaining or promising place. Unless of course there is another overriding imperative. I have known a cat march seemingly oblivious to any risk right into a room and straight onto a special human's lap. He had just come back from a long time away, and for the cat the sheer emotional power and joy of the reunion was more important than anything else.

A cat will very rarely sneak into a room, unless she wants to, and her arrival is often an important announcement. 'I am here, I am back.'

For the fortunate cat, their house territory includes at least one good windowsill. A cat can watch animals, birds and people for hours from a trusted spot. Where possible, any window ledge spot

Cheyenne looking pensive

will also find the sun. If a cat is at home alone for part of the day this windowsill becomes much more important, rather like television might be to you if you live alone. Except it's interactive. If you can watch your cat unobserved, you may well hear her chattering or trilling away. Some people believe this is her trying to imitate potential prey and lure it closer. Others suggest it is merely the equivalent of a human humming when they are happily absorbed in their work. I suspect it is both, often at the same time.

If there is more than one cat in the household the territorial rights to prime spots need to be established. There will be issues about who gets to sit on what chair when, and who is on what side

of the bed — and that's before the other cats are involved. In our small family lounge, Sarah, when she hadn't selected a lap for the evening, had what she made her 'own chair'. It wasn't the biggest or the best chair (Sarah knew she wasn't the total boss; that was Dad) but it was comfortable for her and close to the fire. Should another family member wish to sit there as well, they had to gently slide their way in without disturbing Sarah too much and gently transfer her to their lap. That was allowed. Simply turfing her off the chair clearly was not. My five-year-old self tried in vain to remove her by tipping up the chair but that seldom worked as her claws just gripped on tightly. Opening the door and running noisily into the

kitchen was a shoddy trick and even though Sarah (only) sometimes fell for it she retained the moral high ground, and by implication the territorial rights.

My family has always been allowed by their cats to sleep in their beds. My sister had a precocious Burmese — the elegant Tulip, who every time my wife and I visited claimed both me and my bed as her territory. Just before we went to bed Tulip would slip away and position herself with her tummy upwards, oozing confidence, right in the middle of the pillows, keeping her humans well apart, taking all warmth and attention for herself. Ponk always believes that he has a perfect right to share bedspace and, though the delights of waking up at 3 a.m. with the sound of purring in your ear do wear off, his territorial rights remain unquestioned. Estimates vary but around half of all cat owners allow their cats to sleep on their beds. However, when the bed becomes their territory, woe betide any newcomers. I have heard several stories of new partners being bitten and hissed at by an angry displaced cat. So, if you are bringing someone new into your bed, just be sure that your cat has just as much attention — if not a little more.

Sarah, the Siamese, used to claim a prime spot on the bath stool to help supervise the kids and, while remaining dry, she'd bash at the plastic ducks with her paw. No one else and nothing else was ever allowed on that spot. Towels were pushed off, clothes too, and no human would dare to challenge her. The bath stool's top was made of cork, so it doubled as a useful scratching spot and along with her lounge chair constituted two of her territorial treasures. But Sarah was the only pet in the household.

Physical territory management becomes exponentially more complicated if there is more than one animal in the house. Humans need to get involved a bit too, and not just 'let them sort it out' and see that there are plenty of nice warm, safe places for every cat.

Smart households provide a litter tray for each cat, deftly solving that particular problem, and I have seen some households with additional cat flaps. However, the more entrances there are the more cats that are resident, and security becomes increasingly paramount. For cats, being in a high position provides protection from surprise attacks, superior views and a commanding advantage in any fight. Normally, this is the preference for cats who intend to stay awake, as a secure sleeping space, such as a box, is generally more enclosed. Cats think very carefully about where they place themselves, particularly among each other.

Once there were six cats living in, or mostly outside of, my rustic cottage and each cat had its position around the wooden sun deck. They were all just a few feet apart, the cats who were friendlier with each other staying closer. The two 'most important cats' had their spots at either end of the railings, giving them prime views and defence and attack positions. But every few days the positions changed. Each cat's status hadn't changed much, though this can happen quickly in groups — but what was desirable changed with the weather. The stray grey kitten that had invited herself into the group was no longer cowering under the seats but was atop the railings. The weather had changed, and every cat inverted their position.

If you travel in the less industrialized parts of Europe you will likely find communities of cats in a symbiotic relationship with the locals and tourists. Once in a remote Sicilian village's bistro I saw a couple of hapless kittens that had quietly arrived at my feet, and of course I shared some food with them. The kittens seemed perfectly happy and sedate, and I carried on talking. A couple of minutes later a determined, almost angry tug at my jeans revealed the kitten's mother. She was in effect saying, 'I took you for a soft touch, which is why I left my kittens with you, but you have not fed me yet and that's not the order of things around here — now hurry up.' I complied, so she invited her sister. Other cats looked, but I was now claimed as this family's territory. They even walked me home that night.

Used to tourists, these island cats had a seemingly feral existence with an extensive territorial hierarchy. The village square was bathed in sun and the cats closest to its centre were the more dominant ones. Lesser cats had to content themselves with varying positions further and further down the street. These cats, of course, had adopted some shops as their own, and one small family had made such good friends with the butcher that they adorned his windows during siesta time.

At night the important territories were around the outdoor dining tables and numerous strategies were employed to secure the benefits

of this area. Effectively surrounding an individual or a small group of visitors ensured both food and some kind of protection for the evening. As the provider of food, you took on the boss cat's role and that included defending the family from all intruders be they other hungry cats, clumsy humans or inquisitive dogs. The responsibilities were two way, and your cat group would now seek to protect you. Though seldom lasting a day or two of a tourist's visit, these encounters in cat's territory, which make you in turn part of their territory, can leave lasting memories. At least for the humans. I do wonder if the cats reminisce about past conquests: 'Remember that Englishman? We had his whole steak after Gristlepaw knocked his plate to the ground. Gee, that was a night to remember.'

Typically, male cats have a larger outdoor hunting territory than females, with both genders crossing several miles to leave their 'go away this is my territory' scents and to check if invading cats are attempting the same. Yes, cats hunt for food and if they are making you part of their territory expect food, in varying conditions, to be left for you.

The hunting instinct is much stronger than the power of hunger pangs and well-fed cats make sleeker, strong and fast hunters. They will know what is happening on their territory — mouse hole by mouse hole, bird's nest by bird's nest. They will also know when you are coming home by the unique sound of your car, and they will often be waiting to bring you indoors and make an inventory of the shopping you are taking into the territory.

4

Grooming

A cat's grooming habits are of course an enormous part of their life in every season. In summer saliva helps her cool (remember, cats don't sweat) and her coat is replaced at least once a year but, depending on where she lives, this may be a perpetual, ongoing process.

Seemingly, almost half a cat's waking hours cats are spent grooming themselves and sometimes each other. The little spines in her tongue help sift through the fur and get the protective oils moving, and remove unwelcome visitors, while her damp paws act like cleaning towels. You will notice that a different paw is used for each side of the body. You may always see a clean cat, but with her powerful sense of smell she will notice things about or on herself that you will miss but a predator might not. Cleaning is also a calming process; cats also groom to displace stress. Cats can groom too much and even create small bald patches — this is often a sign of stress and you will need to deal with the cause of this to help stop it.

The act of grooming gives a sense of security and if she has found your lap her security is increased when she is grooming upon you. Don't be offended when your cat immediately starts to groom the moment you have finished stroking or even brushing her; she is just putting her fur back in the right place, thank you.

When your cat grooms you it is more a sign of love and family affection than anything meant to be practical. She knows that you don't have millions of hairs, but you are a member of the family and should be treated accordingly. When cats groom each other the same applies but it's worth noticing that the more dominant the cat the more likely they are to initiate grooming. Notice also that cats grooming each other generally confine themselves to the face and neck areas.

Cat mothers fastidiously groom their kittens from the moment they are born until they can comprehensively do it themselves. Kittens start grooming themselves, and each other, when they are barely a month old, but you will see mother topping up the process and checking that it is done properly and then continue out of affection for as long as they are together.

Keep an eye on older cats who may find it hard to groom as much as they used to — you will need to help out. Ideally you would have got into the daily habit of brushing and grooming your cat yourself from the early days of kittenhood. Just be careful to pay detailed attention to her responses as preferences may change and scratches and bumps you need to know about may have appeared overnight.

One cat who lived with me, Coriander, insisted upon being regularly combed by jumping upon my lap and persistently headbutting my hand until I had got the message. One of her housemates, Bandicoot, used to groom himself noisily and as conspicuously as possible as a form of protest. Remove him from the dining table and he would start to work right in the middle of the floor. Other cats groom when they are feeling stressed or threatened and I have known a few cats who have attempted to make some sense of my hair by grooming me.

Estimates vary as to how much of their awake time cats spend grooming, but if yours spends well over a third of her time doing this she would not be unusual.

5

Where a cat sits

Cheyenne in the bin

Deciding where to sit isn't as easy for a cat as it probably is for you and me. A cat weighs up the conflicting needs of warmth, comfort, security, the ability to be near you and/or smell you, and being somewhere they can watch for intruders and prey. If it's somewhere close to things to investigate and play with, so much the better. Cats can sit for a very long time, sometimes awake, and appreciate the ability to gently switch in and out of sleep, so location matters most of all.

The more other animals are around the greater the desirability of high places. Cats are so much better at climbing than other animals and a higher position is easily defended. High positions also afford the best views and you will find when in a house with many cats that the more dominant the cat the higher their normal sitting position is. That is of course if they are not closest to you, or better still on your lap.

Cats like privacy as well, which is something that a high window ledge can never provide. Cardboard boxes are much sought after for this reason — they can hide in them, and they are warm. If you think your cat is sending you a message by sitting in a box, they are, and it will be along the lines of 'Leave me alone and turn the heating up'. Unless of course it's a kitten, who can explore and then get

stuck in a tissue box and go to sleep while someone else sorts it out for them in time.

Dark, warm places are particularly desirable sitting and sleeping spots. An older home I once lived in had its sheets and towels stored next to the hot water boiler, which made a soft, dark and luxuriant hideaway. Whenever we couldn't find the cat, she was normally shut in there and never too pleased to have her secret hideaway rediscovered.

While your cat is likely to love being in your home and around you, she also wants her own privacy. Some grooming is best done in private; she also wants to sleep without being disturbed, and always be safe from any real or imagined prey. Hiding is a useful hunting technique and a particularly good sport when she is pretending not to want to be found. So, you will find your cat in all sorts of

extraordinary places, but notice that only a few of many hiding places are ever used again after you have found them.

Cats also like sitting on things associated with you. My sister has a cat, Lightning, who likes to sit on top of my head. Knowing that he will never get an invitation, Lightning gently stages his move. First he will look at me pretending to be impressed. I think Lightning is seeing somebody he likes. But actually all he cares about now is the big, warm ball otherwise known as my head. He will always secure an invitation to my lap. From there he moves up to my chest, purring away so I think he is a looking at me adoringly. I am fooled and he goes further up to purr in my ear, and while I am working out if that's a good thing or not Lightning settles right across my head, knowing full well that attempting to remove him risks at the very least accidental scratches. So Lightning stays there for as long as he wants. Which is longer than I would choose.

When he is not on my head, Lightning will settle for the book I am reading or the exact part of the newspaper. I like to think that it's my scent he is attracted to, but I suspect it's a way to ensure that he gets the appropriate amount of attention and is also claiming me, and anything associated with me, as his territory. It's not that Lightning's brother, Thunder, the only other cat in the house, is going to be particularly impressed with this approach. A key part of Thunder's life strategy is to headbutt anything and everything that Lightning has touched so his mark is there instead. When he smells this, Lightning must establish himself all over again, and this process can repeat itself over days.

Thunder's favourite siting position is in the middle of a narrow stairway at the darkest point in the house. Like many cats he is fond

Lightning aged one or two years

of 'his' place and will not give it up without considerable persuasion and a worthwhile exchange. After all, he has deduced that this is *the* place for him and has probably fought with Lightning to establish it as his own. So when I am lumbering upstairs with a big heavy suitcase, Thunder is not keen on moving. It normally plays out along these lines. Thunder sees me coming up the stairs and is outraged that I am potentially blocking his view of more interesting

Totoro, the garden helper

things and, worse still, I may want him to move. He turns away and pretends not to see me. I puff up to one stair below where he is sitting and say hello. Thunder then looks at me despairingly but brightens up for a moment to headbutt the suitcase — there! It's part of his territory now and he cheers up. It's a big case but I manage to lift it past him and head towards my bedroom. Thunder follows, waiting to see what's in the case. As I open it, he moves in. I try talking to him but now he is too busy to chat as there are new things to smell, scuff up, explore and play with. An hour later I am still not unpacked, and Thunder is fast asleep in the case while Lightning, who has come to check what's going on, decides to sit right at my feet because there is obviously going to be something interesting happening quite soon, even if it's only him eating my shoelaces.

Where cats sit in the wild on their hunting missions is determined by similar requirements to their needs at home. I have seen cats on the top of solitary fence posts, astride narrow gates, in high tree branches, on truck roofs (which can cause inevitable mayhem when the perch decides to move), hiding in shrubs, and asleep next to warm compost heaps. Exploring and finding a good perch can lead to difficulties, the most well-known of which is that the cat gets stuck up a tree — her claws make climbing up easy, but going down is harder. However, on nearly all occasions (and I stress nearly) the cat, thought to be stuck and probably complaining to you very volubly about it, is quite capable of getting down on her own. What she needs is peace. Children and dogs and adult

Cheyenne in a barrow

humans with suggestions and opinions are not going to help her.

Cats can be very private creatures. They are also very mindful of their own dignity. They will normally know how to get out of a tight spot given time and privacy. No self-respecting cat is going to demonstrate an ungainly bottom-first scrabble slide and claw, scrabble and slide again routine in front of you. But if you watch very carefully in a truly hidden way, this is what you will see — that is, of course, if you haven't already tried to call out the fire brigade.

Sometimes cats sit right next to you for no more obvious reason than sharing quiet company. Peaceful time is a precious part of a cat's life; you should be flattered should your cat choose to share this with you.

6

Where cats go and what happens at night

Cats go to the same places indoors and outdoors, so if yours goes missing she may not be hard to find. You will know your cat's character — if she is shy and centred around home and safety she will probably be quite close, and if she is not in any of her normal places she is probably in the nearest safe place to home. However, if she is a big exploring, gregarious type who likes humans, you will need to cast your net far and wide, but in the directions you know she has been before. If you have more than one cat it's important that you understand all your cats, not just the indoor ones. You need to know where they go when they leave your lap. Not just because that will help find them should they go missing and want to be found, but knowing what they do will at the very least mean you don't get strange people coming around and claiming your cat as their own.

There is the story of a plump red cat called Rufus who adopted Peter, a man with a big fireplace and a generous nature with food. Rufus was elusive during the day, meowing himself out at around 7 a.m. and meowing himself back in again around 8 p.m. Peter was pleased to have Rufus in his life; they were, after all, both single males seemingly without many people in life. Until one day some six months into the arrangement, six-year-old Emily and eight-year-old Olivia knocked on Peter's door and asked if he wouldn't mind being ever so kind and stop feeding 'their Bertie'. Bertie/Rufus was sprawled at home right across the fireplace and, pretending he didn't want to be there any more, walked out with the girls. It was three days before he came back.

The Cat Protection Society in New South Wales, Australia, informed me about a project, The Cats of Erskineville, which involved a team of artists, vets and technologists putting tracking and night vision cameras on cats to see what they got up to after

dark. One of the 'stars' was an elegant cat called Jewels, who patiently waited every night for her family to go to bed and turn their lights off. She then went next door and upstairs to join a male cat. Jewels' waiting for her household to go quiet suggests that she sensed they might not have approved of her nocturnal sojourns.

Another cat, Fish, seemingly went hunting for bugs. Kiki patrolled the roof tops at the end of her street. Suki filled a basket with socks and men's underwear she gathered on her travels, and handsome Billy kept a watchful eye on the trees, perhaps in case something climbed down them without his permission. Jeff the

Dude seemed to hang around collecting pats and compliments from passers-by but he had been known to come home in the small hours smelling of lady's perfume.

All the cats in this exercise had their travels mapped over a 24-hour period. Erskineville is a quiet, contained community so some overlapping of patrols and territories seems inevitable. Yet just how social cats are (and it's not just about mating) was surprising. Some areas were visited at different times by six cats, and the exercise also let us see how cats chat with each other in regular haunts.

Mating and fighting may attract more attention but desexed cats make great friends with each other. By and large, cats get along just fine. My nocturnal lane cat had plenty of friends, and all around the world cats gather in clowders, clutters, clusters and, my favourite of the collective nouns, 'a glaring of cats'.

7

Breeding

As more people keep cats, and in turn some of these go feral, controlling cat numbers has become a focus of attention. But there remains a significant resistance to neutering. Cats can start breeding when they are a little over two months old, and within a lifespan of possibly ten years or more a single cat can produce over 150 kittens. Cats can be on heat for several days in a cycle that can rapidly repeat during a mating season, which often starts before the warm weather and ends when it gets cold. It's a stressful period for the cat and is yet another reason for her and her likely mates to be spayed.

Typically, a female cat may be pursued by up to six suitors. If they are all announcing their presence — which they do loudly, and which is known as caterwauling — it will be a very noisy period with a lot of additional spraying and fighting. The actual act of intercourse can often last no more than ten seconds. Male cats are sexually ready by the time they are three months old, and as they develop they are more aggressive with other males and spend more time outdoors. Male cats are interested in reproduction both in play, when they practise the neck grip on their litter buddies of either gender before they are capable, and in their dotage when they are past it.

When a female cat is on heat you may see her rolling around and rubbing onto objects more than usual, and you will hear a lot more from her as she incessantly demands both attention and to be let out. As the pregnancy progresses she will be keeping closer to home ground and will be finding safe places to give birth. Gestation is approximately over 60 days and your cat is likely to come back on heat within two months of giving birth.

A cat's litter could have kittens from more than one father, but they are all treated the same. Most cats are great parents, and for the first month of their lives kittens are fully tended to. Thereafter, the kittens rapidly achieve independence. They are then very quickly full of curiosity and fun.

There are over 100 million pet cats in the United States alone. They are deemed to be responsible for the death of over a billion birds each year. The US government euthanizes millions of feral cats but, as with the rest of the world, until most domestic cats are neutered

the problems will persist. Neutered cats have a smaller hunting range than non-neutered cats and generally stay closer to home in all ways. The obstacles to neutering include cost (or more often the perception of the cost), ignorance of the fate and damage caused by abandoned kittens, and getting around to it too late. Cats who live in households with other kinds of pets are a little less likely to be neutered than those from cat-only households. The more the 'owner' is cat-focused the greater care taken, or so it seems, and a great way of looking after cats in general is to ensure that they are neutered — that way, cats have a longer, easier life.

8

Hunting

Totoro in the flowers

Though geography and the relative comforts of home influence a cat's approach to its wider territory, the love of hunting and exploration can provide a greater stimulus for action.

Some cats can travel for days away from home absorbing adventures and return looking decidedly the worse for wear, while other cats are not even keen on leaving the house. The nature of these preferences does not voluntarily change; a happy house cat is unlikely to become a big warrior hunter; and while a big hunter may stay closer to home as the years pass, don't be surprised to see old preferences re-emerge from time to time.

I used to have a major hunter cat when I grew up on a fruit farm in England's Southwest. Sarah, my father's much-loved Siamese Seal Point, was normally easy to spot. She used to vanish for days, and once when she had gone too long for comfort and fearing the worst, I walked out a long way looking for her. We met soon enough, and it was obvious to her that I was the one out of my habitat. Though Sarah was unimpressed by my refusal to go home across freshly sown, muddy farmland, she seemed content enough to have her worlds of a comfortable home and big hunts merge.

Some major exploring cats don't come home for weeks or even months, until something calls them back to their other lives. I have noticed that cats who live among just one or two others at home are more likely to wander for longer periods than those who live among a larger group. There are status levels to protect in households with other cats and animals, so being gone too long might risk losing the right to that hard-earned perch on the high windowsill. If there is just one human the cat feels immediately responsible for, and no one to delegate to, they are unlikely to be gone for unexpectedly long periods. Cats take their responsibilities seriously. Just realize that they alone decide what those responsibilities are. They have decided what yours are too.

I have heard several stories of cats not being in the slightest bit interested in the mice and rats they were invited into the home to deal with, and I have known many cats to be quite indignant when I have come home earlier or later than I was supposed to. Cats enjoy the routines they choose. My sister's cats were 'outraged' when Covid lockdowns denied them exclusive full run of the house during regular working hours, and pointed her to the front door.

If a maturing cat starts taking a greater interest in being out and about, try to remember the total amount of time they are away. You might find this gradually increases. You may think they are happy exploring new territory. Maybe, but also, you have gradually been trained to not worry about them being away for longer and longer periods. So, what started as three hours can become five hours, then a whole day; then a day and a night, then two days and one night, and so forth. You will of course now have to compete for your cat's attention. Though, as in all feline matters, there are no hard and fast rules; female cats, for example, seem to be more interested in hunting than their brothers.

Many well-fed domestic cats, allowed outdoors, will be out and about hunting for up to three hours a day. Feral cats, who must hunt, are thought to do so for up to twelve hours each day. When there are not rodents or other vermin to deal with in their close home territory, the amount of earnestness in the domestic cat's endeavours will depend upon how many other distractions there are that day, the weather, how much they feel like giving you a present or if they are seeking a change of diet.

Some cats (like Suki in Erskineville, who liked to collect men's underwear and socks) have a habit of collecting things, and occasionally their habits are sprawled across the newspaper. Dennis in Bedfordshire, England, has his own line of printed T-shirts emblazoned with 'Dennis stole my pants', such is the renown of his thievery, with funds going to a local cat rescue organization. Dennis has also been known to steal designer polo shirts and shoes. The beautifully named Snorri Sturluson, from Portland, Oregon, has a penchant for shoes and eventually his neighbours learnt to check Snorri's Instagram account to see if their missing shoes were there. Angel, from New Zealand's South Island, started off her life of crime with the humble tea bag but quickly scaled up to underwear, shoes and more. There are many similar stories.

Kittens are often given toys to play with and treat the toys as prey. Then, as hunting instincts loom larger in adulthood, and if there is no need to catch food as there is plenty of it already deboned at home, prey becomes something else. A nice smelly sock might be easier to catch than a rabbit anyway, and you don't often get screamed at for coming home with a sock. Given that cats' hunting habits have catastrophic impacts upon some forms of wildlife, finding ways to get cats to hunt toys and socks could be good for all concerned. In many countries the habitat used by native animals is shrinking as humans, and their cats, move into their territories and the impact of cats is becoming more noticeable and discussed. Some regional councils have attempted to put local rules in place restricting cat ownership because of the damage caused. These have largely failed and not just because the ever-growing number of feral cats cannot read — the issue is far more in the public eye than it has ever been.

Cats have always been appreciated by humans for their hunting abilities. Ancient Egyptians even worshipped them, and the cats repaid them by killing snakes. When humans changed from living in nomadic to settled cultures and needed grain stores, it was the cats who kept the rodents at bay. Large congregations of mice, warm and safe fireplaces, and outlandish behaviour made humans interesting to cats. Humans, for their part, appreciated the cats' abilities to control rodents, and the two species started to travel together.

Our level of respect towards cats has seen many changes over the years, but their practical value was once more realized when the Industrial Revolution led to the creation of huge warehouses and

factories with a variety of stores right across the world, and cats took up official pest control positions. Wherever there are rodents, cats are needed. Even today you may well find a cat in a bourbon or whiskey distillery, as well as doing useful work on farms.

Subverting and changing cats' habit of hunting alongside humans, which stretches back thousands of years, will require thinking far more creative than often experienced in local council chambers. Cat lovers also need to help more by recognizing that wildlife destruction is a problem. Indeed, caring members of the cat-owning community are already actively working to reduce the damage.

೧๏

Cats are always playful — but when playful, puss probably wants you to know that she is not just wandering around sniffing outdoors; she is up to serious business. Except when she is not.

Cats can get away with a lot of private time when they are hunting and they clearly must not be disturbed. All puss needs to do is to pretend to crouch and you know the game is afoot. Cats catch things probably as regularly as they want to and can eat an enormous variety of birds, bugs, reptiles, rats, mice and their cousins, frogs and toads, rabbits, hares and much else besides, including fish and indeed can try out anything interesting for taste.

A cat's instinct to hunt can easily take her over 2 kilometres (around 1½ miles) on a normal day and regularly cover several hectares. Nocturnal patrols tend to take in a slightly larger area; cats are well tuned to the Earth's magnetic field (they will know about a thunderstorm before you do) and find their way home from much greater distances than are covered in a routine hunt.

Catches of animals well over a third of the cat's size are not uncommon, and just about everyone who lives with a hunting cat has a story about the big things that have been bought home. I grew up on a farm and well remember the panic in the household full of burly blokey boys when Sarah, the Siamese, brought in an angry, screaming stoat in her mouth, dropping it in the kitchen. Sarah then feigned boredom with the whole exercise and disappeared, leaving the rest of us to somehow deal with it. Sarah was fond of catching extra-large rabbits and the occasional seagull,

Lightning eating autumn leaves

and a seemingly endless procession of decapitated mice was strewn all over the house.

Sarah, like other cats, was often seen playing with her prey — particularly mice. The poor thing would be thrown up in the air, land with a thud and scurry off in escape, only to be quickly caught again and hurled back into the ether again and again. I have no doubt that Sarah enjoyed this and that the mice did not. With mice, some people say that this kind of capture is neither deliberately cruel nor playful, but necessary. Apparently, a mouse is best killed by a sharp severing bite to the back of its neck. Getting the mouse into the difficult position to do this explains the constant playing and throwing around. Apparently. Yet other animals like to play with their prey. Killer Whales have been known to play catch with seals and, like cats' behaviour, there is more going on than simply disorienting and positioning prey before the kill.

As we were supposed to believe with the stoat, Sarah could genuinely get bored with the same not-dead-yet mouse, and a few escaped. One took up residence in my box of building blocks and even bred there, and Sarah, generally a superb hunter, never seemed to bother about that new family. She had already established that she was the boss with them and there were plenty of others to deal with.

Cats can look upon their entire household — you included — as kittens needing to be taught how to hunt and are introduced when in the litter to a variety of living play. Then comes the leap and the swat and the throw, and we are supposed to watch and follow. I have seen cats playing with young children and crouching as if teaching them this vital technique. But then again, the cats could have been preparing themselves for a big leap to safety.

A hunting cat's planning and patience is completely integrated into its entire lifestyle. A cat will know its territory so intimately that it is likely to notice any subtle change. The digging of a tiny mouse hole, a new or enlarged bird's nest, even rabbit, mouse or rat droppings not will go unobserved during a cat's daily patrols. For weeks or even months the cat will return to the holes and nests to see what is going on and be ready to strike. Then, as cat owners have all too often and painfully seen, an entire nest and family can be 'harvested' by puss and possibly deposited in your house. Or, if you're lucky, just on your doorstep.

⁓

Not all cats like hunting. Of course, many are not given the opportunity to, but some who are just don't see the point in it and prefer the comforts of home. Why go off into wet pastures or close to smelly rat holes when there is central heating and food and admiration on tap at home and computers to wreck?

There is no accurate way of knowing how many cats prefer this lifestyle. Of the eighteen cats studied in the Erskineville project only three opted to stay at home all the time, and just six were known hunters. Other surveys have pointed to a much higher ratio of hunters and geography clearly plays a part. Generally, cat 'owners' underestimate the amount of time their cat spends hunting. A South Australian visual survey found that many owners believed their cat was safely in the house for the night and were astonished to see footage of their cats being out and about.

Cats like to explore, to hunt and satisfy their curiosity about the world around them, and simple expedients like closed doors and locked cat flaps are unlikely to reliably stop them from doing this. I once had a pair of cats live with me in the lush outer suburbs of Auckland's West Coast in New Zealand. Ms Coriander and Mr Bandicoot had both been rescued as struggling kittens by an animal shelter, and nobody knew anything about their background.

Coriander was a highly effective hunter, despite having an almost luminescent pale-blue coat. Conversely, the earth-brown, brilliantly camouflaged Bandicoot was either hopeless or not interested. It took me a while to work this out. Bandicoot was, at best, keen on exaggerating his skills. About six months after they had both settled in with me, dead animals started appearing on the door mat. I lived on a cliff edge and Coriander would watch me with that air of mystified 'I wouldn't believe he could do this unless I had seen it myself' disdain that cats retain for humans, as I threw rats over the cliff into the deep bush. I would then try to make it up to Coriander, telling her how clever and useful she was, but of course Ms was 'above all of that'. I would get on with my business and about 20 minutes later another dead rat would appear on the mat, with Bandicoot looking very pleased with himself and expecting attention with praise and a hero's status. He got away with it, for a while at least, confirming for Coriander that life was unfair.

Eventually I twigged: Bandicoot was simply retrieving Coriander's catches and claiming them as his own. As the years progressed, he became more subtle, sometimes bringing days-old carcasses right into the house. I never thought he caught anything himself — he was more of an explorer cat and I heard many reports of him miles away from home. But I still don't think he hunted. He was, though, like many cats, tremendously good at shredding my sofas and easy chairs, so his back legs were strong and his claws sharp and ready.

A cat's hunting techniques of stalking, silently and secretly getting into crouching and pouncing position, are well known, as are their exceptional sense of smell, their binocular vision, their ultra-perceptive whiskers and startling turn of speed. But if that should not be enough there is guile, plain cleverness and immense patience. Sarah employed a technique I have seen snakes use in Australia, which is to lie concealed at the foot of a bush, her excited swishing tail moving the bush's branches and leaves to excite and confuse birds who, when they'd come for a close look, could quickly become prey.

Cats and tigers share nearly all their DNA and a cat's stalking technique seems almost identical to a tiger's. Common to both is a quiet stalk followed by a short-distance ambush of immense speed and a bite to the neck. Being more settled than tigers, cats can patiently watch the same place for weeks on end before bringing home prey. Sarah used to watch a family of moles for weeks before bringing them all into the house one by one. The moles were confused but unharmed, though Sarah seemed affronted when I returned them to the garden, and the exercise was repeated a few times each summer. Cats have binocular-type vision and can see over short distances with almost total accuracy. Their vision tends towards being more black and white than ours, so they have much less information to deal with and, when hunting, they can focus just on their prey.

Tigers and lions are reputedly only successful in about one in every five hunts. The smaller the cat, the higher the success ratio. If the cat's mother brought home prey to her kittens, she would have imitated the kittens' sounds and showed them how to swat, pounce and play. If you can watch your cat preparing for the kill, note how there is something like a dance in the final moments. Although an individual cat, like Sarah, can bring home the most eclectic assortment of prey, many cats persist with either mice and other rodents or small (-ish) birds. These aptitudes or skills are probably passed on by the mother.

When they are just a month old, wild and feral kittens are given live prey to play with. This suggests, of course, that those cats who kill socks and collect other inanimate objects were probably separated from their mother before hunting lessons had begun.

Coriander's favourite technique was a blistering speed ambush; in a microsecond what was a small, shimmering blue haze became a bolt of devastating light. No long prowls and lengthy stalks for her — Ms Coriander's range was safely within our urban driveway's boundary. If there were no rats to catch it was mice, and if they weren't co-operating then birds; if they weren't available, cheeky flower heads that needed to be decapitated from their stalks. Whatever it was, Coriander moved so fast that nothing would have known what had happened to it.

In general, I have found that, like lions, female cats are the more prolific and efficient hunters. Bandicoot never seemed to want to catch anything that wasn't already dead and Mr Punk's technique is

novel but not always effective. Ponk eases himself onto tiny ledges and micro spaces where not even an intelligent creature could believe a cat would lurk, and carries out tail-flying dancing ambushes from there. He was hiding in the shadow of a small stairwell once, when he leapt upon a moth that had settled four steps away. The moth must have been a little alarmed as it fluttered up to one higher stair level. Ponk has developed his 'attack from unlikely places' technique into an art form by practising it when birds are distracted by the presence of humans. His human family unwittingly provide cover for him and they are just as startled as the bird when, from seemingly nowhere (an impossibly narrow window ledge) Ponk flings himself gleefully over their heads towards the bird. When he misses, Ponk makes it clear he was only practising jumping anyway.

I did see Ponk capture a bird once. It wasn't clear who was most surprised — the humans who shouted in alarm; the poor bird; me, who happened to be looking; or Ponk himself, who was so surprised that he immediately let the poor sparrow fly indignantly off.

Hunting is of course the joyful, unfettered exercise of instinct, and if something to play with and then either eat or donate is the outcome, so much the better.

9

Food

While hunting is not always about food, getting fed becomes a very serious matter at home. Most cats will quickly train their owners — or more accurately 'staff' — as to what kind of things to feed them and when. The rules are uncomplicated: the *cat* can change the feeding places and time, and demand food from, for example, your own dinner plate, but *you* cannot vary the time and regular feeding places. For humans, food is often tied to family and social activities. For cats it most certainly isn't. A cat will share its plate with another feline, or sometimes (though rarely) another small creature it deems deserving, but only on its own terms. That means not on yours! Cats like to eat lot of small meals, regularly grazing like some people believe humans should. But while it may be fine for you to skip a meal or eat much later than normal, for the cat, this is unacceptable behaviour. Meal times are the clock of life itself and must be kept to whether your cat was properly fed just half an hour beforehand. It's the ritual and pattern that's important. A cat's body clock is a precision instrument. If she is normally fed at 6 p.m. you will be reminded of this by 5.45 p.m.

If your cat demands feeding at meal times when she cannot be hungry, she is requiring you to navigate through life the way she expects you to. There are, though, plenty of examples of over-fed secure cats who are not necessarily greedy — rather, they are running to a routine. I have seen this process managed in a brilliant way. A friend rescued, fell in love and shared her home with a couple of street cats in Shanghai and on leaving managed, after a long sojourn in the United States, to bring them home to Australia. After so much change and upset it's not surprising that they were particularly keen on routines. Anna and Cleo required feeding at 5.30 a.m. and 5 p.m. come what may. But my friend has learnt that if the cats have in effect been recently fed, perhaps while she was preparing a meal, all that is required is the act of putting something in their bowl, and as they are not actually hungry a couple of small dry biscuits served by hand in front of Anna and Cleo demonstrated that their world remained in order.

We have seen that a cat likes to be fed both when he wants to be and when you ought to be feeding him. He would like to eat whatever you have that he likes and some of the food he approves of that you regularly supply. His tastes of course are subject to change and for no obvious reason he can cease liking his favourite brand of cat food and refuse to even look at it again. Similarly, what he rejected last month is now the only food he is truly interested in. So what's going on here?

Just like humans, cats' food preferences change with the seasons and whatever else is going on in their lives, and the mix used in commercially available cat foods can change sufficiently to alter its appeal. However, I think the real reason that cats are known to be fussy and picky eaters has less to do with taste and attending to

their body's needs than it has to do with what we understand as the simple concept of being fed. Except, for a cat this is not simple at all. Unless you are a kitten, being fed really isn't a natural thing for cats. Unlike dogs, cats need to comprehensively oversee their own destiny. Cats will never delegate the responsibility for their food to anyone. Rather, they train and manage you and your household to provide what they want. Cats have been managing humans for millennia and their techniques are derived a little from their parenting style and a lot from their hunting style.

First, they discover where their prey is. Your cat knows what's in your shopping and where you put it. Many cats will always be in the kitchen when food is being prepared so they know what's where and what is likely to be good. Second, they need to get access to it. Looking at a tin of food isn't going to make it open. They need tools and you or any other compliant human will be made to do the job. This is not to say that a cat might come running at you with a tin opener in its mouth; that's far too undignified. Rather, you are now the proxy for the prey. You are going to be stalked. If you are not already in the kitchen, your cat will locate you. Believe me, they always know where you are. They know what they want to eat, they know what's available and where you are, and will move right next to you.

So far this process would not normally take as long as 30 seconds. Third, your cat must now capture you and bring you 'home' to the food rather than drop you on the mat like other prey. You would have seen lots of tools used here. It's very rare for a cat to go straight to the killer bite — but it's been known, so you would be wise to pay attention. Normally, the stare is employed in the early moves. This hypnotic gaze has led to the demise of millions of mice, who have fallen victim to it as they've peeped out of their holes. As Ponk knows, I can't last beyond this point and he needs to do no more.

But other humans can be made of sterner stuff. A gentle pounce onto an unprepared lap or a flying leap into someone's arms gets their attention. Now the stare can be put into effect at close range. If this doesn't get you rushing to the kitchen your cat will be surprised. Possibly exasperated. Because with all this attention you should have worked out that it's near their normal feeding time.

If you are remaining obdurate, specialized tools for hunting humans come into play. Fourth, she will start making a noise: no kitten-like meows in these conditions, your cat will unleash their high-frequency cry, which somehow conveys a compelling sense of urgency you are hard-wired to respond to. At this stage it's more about shepherding you than hunting.

So now you are in the kitchen. What is your cat going to be served? How your cat responds to what you feed it, and in turn to you, is related to the amount of effort it took to get you to put the food onto their plate. No cat would happily go through the full palaver described above for a handful of kibbles. How much effort would your cat put into hunting a mere moth? So, if you have been hunted down you had better deliver the good stuff. And here is where the fun can really start. The cat knows that you are not going to let her go hungry for long, and she also knows that anything you are having is legitimately hers. Cats are generally not keen on any kind of change, so when a commercial or local cat food is accepted and you stick with it, it's reasonable to assume she will continue to like it. This can go on for a long time. Then suddenly it can change. Generally, after you have bought the next month's stock. She could have decided that life was too easy and you may be taking her for granted. Alternatively, of course, the manufacturer might have changed the mix. Or just like humans she occasionally feels like a change. You will always be clear about your cat's opinion on what you feed her.

Every cat has a somewhat different set of protocols over what and where to eat. Chloe refuses to eat anything that does not come out of a tin with 'cat food' plastered all over it. Sarah was the opposite, indignantly shaking her foot vigorously at most things that were offered. Arran and Skye had to pick up bits and roll them around the floor until they were satisfied they were dead. Then they would pick up the bits, return them to the plates we had put them in, and we would clean up the kitchen and look perplexed. Thunder and Lightning must have learnt speed eating from a large dog: they inhale their food so quickly that they genuinely cannot believe they have eaten and immediately restart the hunting process after each meal. Bandicoot would walk all around his plate purring contentedly, then without eating anything walk away for a few seconds and come back to check that, yes, his food was still there. He would then purr at it a bit more then slowly eat it all. Bandicoot was always fastidious — there was never anything dropped on the floor and his plate was always licked perfectly clean.

Coriander is the only cat I have known to be fussier about where she ate than what she was eating; most cats go to the same place where the bowls are all set up for them. Coriander used to start there, then, looking fixedly at me, go to where she wanted her bowl moved to and meow loudly until I had done it. She could change her mind during the process and get me to carry her bowl further and further away for her. Coriander was keeping her food safe from predators, not Bandicoot, and other cats have been known to try to cover up the bowl to hide it.

Everyone who has shared life with cats will have their own stories of feline fussiness, which can at times be extreme. There is Purdey, a famous London pub cat who is known to only eat gourmet food, which certainly does not include mice. Cats can over-feed, though in general they don't, or are just not allowed to, and even most pub and club cats are not 'remarkably' fat like T.S. Eliot's Bustopher Jones — but many can be as discerning. Cats have been known, especially when establishing their rules in a new home, to almost starve themselves in their insistence on only eating one kind of food.

Cats do share their food, when it suits them, and some people may even believe the story of the courtier imprisoned in the Tower of London being kept alive by the jailhouse cat delivering him pigeons. When dead prey is dropped at your door, as happens to most cats' staff, you are probably also being fed. Cats expect to share your food too (well, it's only fair) but sharing your food is quite different to the things that must happen at the proper feeding times. She cares for you, and you must show her the same courtesy. The cat will, of course, get to discover different foods this way and this may lead to different demands. Originally, all cats were wild and then they travelled alongside humans with geography, seasons, health and activity levels changing their diet. So a cat's inbuilt propensity to try new flavours can be satisfied by what you are eating. Of course, there will be some foods you eat that she absolutely adores and insists upon. However, cats recognize that there is limited availability and, unless they are of the more determined kind, most cats will give up demanding smoked salmon if it has not appeared after a week or so; they will assume it's out of season.

10

Sounds

Cats are intensely emotional creatures who see, hear and sense infinitely more than humans do. They are always calibrating what is happening in life, and in one way or another are constantly communicating with you. Even if a cat appears diffident, he is communicating — if a cat is ever disinterested in you he will have found his privacy — so when he is pointedly ignoring you something is being conveyed.

The most normal sound is the purr. Someone compared a cat's purr to a human's smile: generally lovely, friendly, warm and sincere but occasionally ironic, cynical and a fabrication. All cat lovers know the purr and the harmonics are reputedly good for his bone structure and are soothing for you as well as him. When anxious or even stressed a cat will start to purr. Normally, though, a purr conveys, through its decibel level, degrees of happiness. I have known cats to purr at their food bowl, at likely living prey, at me and other cat lovers and even at the familiar goldfish — though that, of course, could be seen as prey.

Purrs can be loud. *The Guinness Book of Records* has had entries over 67 decibels — that's similar to traffic noise and your vacuum cleaner, and is in fact about the same level as a robust human conversation. Yet most purrs are around 25 decibels, a similar level to a child's whisper.

> A cat's rage is beautiful, burning with pure cat flame,
> all its hair standing up and crackling blue sparks,
> eyes blazing and sputtering.

William S. Burroughs

The opposite of the purr is the hiss. This short angry sound is normally used between cats as an 'I have run out of tolerance and will shortly attack' warning. The same level of venom and fury can be expressed to humans doing the wrong thing. Cats can hiss at strangers in their house who have not been properly introduced, and those who have for misbehaving. Cats like other beings to be orderly

and predictable. Children causing a ruckus never get hissed at but adults being noisy, especially in the middle of the night, often do.

There is no vocal prelude to a hiss. But there is a certainty that unless the aberrant behaviour ceases pretty much instantly, an attack will follow. Perhaps wisely, cats hiss at each other far more than at humans. There has been some speculation that as early domesticated cats were venerated and encouraged by Egyptians for their snake-killing abilities, cats learnt to use a snake's noise in the same weapon-like manner. When you see kittens playing with each other you will hear them attempt to hiss. At just two weeks old kittens can hiss, which is a whole week ahead of their being able to purr and, being that small and frail, the ability to pretend to be something dangerous is likely to be a valuable resource. A hissing cat also shows its teeth and tigers hiss in the same way when they feel insecure or threatened.

> There is no past, present or future; there is only meow, right meow, and what you do with your one shot at life.
>
> *Aaron Dennis*

There is a general understanding that though meows occur between mothers and kittens, meowing is predominantly used by cats to talk to humans. Sadly, humans often misunderstand the meow. Witness the fact that should you have ever said a bitchy remark in your life, it is likely that a friend would have said 'Meow' to you as if you were being cat-like. But cats are not often like that and they experience every emotion and feeling in the world, so there are a lot of meows. Let's go through a day of them.

At some ridiculously early hour many a self-respecting cat will quietly announce herself with a little meow just to check that you know she is entitled to jump on your bed. Typically, she will take care to make sure you have gone to sleep and then start noisily grooming. You toss and turn, and she responds with a gently remonstrative meow — pitched a little higher and drawn out a little longer than her greeting. You go back to sleep and she waits incredibly patiently for at least three minutes, then decides that you must stop sleeping your life away and do something useful. Actually, something very useful — feeding her. This is normally announced with a double meow: the first sounds almost like a question, 'Are you awake now?' and the second a protest, 'Well, you should be.' You begin to clamber out of bed and she goes to the edge just to jump down, and you may well get a third burst, this being a single meow: 'Well, get on with it please.' She will precede you into the kitchen and take a strategic position between the cupboard or fridge and the food bowl. Now, if she is extra hungry and if you have kept her waiting you may get the machine gun 'meow meow meow', which is little more than 'Hurry up hurry up hurry up'. But often you will get a simple soft meow by the time you have opened the cupboard, which is the nearest you will get to 'Thank you for doing the right thing'.

Then, if you live on your own there may well be a quick meow which just says 'door' and once opened you may have at least two minutes before you hear a loud double meow 'open up'. If there are no other humans around to check upon, you may then get a soft sleepy meow as she finds your chair and goes to sleep.

Two hours later you will likely hear the 'I am here and okay; where are you?' inquisitive meow. Then, if you do respond you will likely hear a softer, less certain more mew-like meow, which to you says, 'I am cute; come and give me some attention'. I have had cats who, when happy, leave out the M altogether, emitting a sound sometimes more like 'oof' than 'eow'. Oofs are meows of intimate satisfaction and approval, and never loud enough to be heard by any more than one person. This means she is completely happy and another sleep may be forthcoming. The next meow can be both inquisitive and hopeful yet demanding, 'Are you ready to play, because I am?' All goes well until someone more important comes home and all you will hear is meow meow meow meow meow meow — 'Me, me, pay attention to me' — at which point the new arrival has no choice but to accede to the cat's demands.

As you go your separate ways in the house there may well be quiet for a while. The next meow will be 'I am here; are you?' If you ignore this, the next meow will be quiet but with a hint of a snarl, 'huh'.

You can of course decide whether to respond to a meow. Some people suggest that you don't, but quite why you would share life with a cat and not want to communicate with it is beyond my comprehension.

To truly communicate with your cat you are going to need to look at her very carefully. Like humans, most feline communication is not verbal at all, and you can be fairly sure that your cat will understand your body language. However, the more your cat meows the more doubtful she is of your ability to understand her non-verbal cues. More on feline body language later, for right now the next barrage of meows is likely to come.

You ignored her last little 'huh' so maybe as much as ten minutes later there is a pair of high-pitched meow meows: 'Where, where [are you]?' Ignore this and the volume and distress level will shoot up proportionally. A distressed cat's meow can quickly progress into a yowl, and with either added age or stress a yowl can become a yodel. You don't want to hear these sounds; they are not made by a happy cat.

Once rescued from her isolation and anxiety and again made the rightful centre of attention, your cat is likely to give you a little meow (thanks) and go happily on her way to her private areas. One cat I had always meowed loudly by her cat flap before going out hunting: 'It's me. I am out for a while, don't worry — just behave yourselves and be here when I get back.'

11

Cats with jobs

You will often hear about cats being employed. They run some American bookstores, supervise British public houses and their breweries, run trains and stations, help Manhattan building 'supers', keep theatres pest-free and more besides. However, despite these almost conventional-sounding roles, most normal employment practices do not apply. For a start, the cat decides what the job is, whether or not you knew there was a vacancy; they determine the working hours and conditions; and they are the ones asking the questions at the interview. Despite this potentially unpromising start to a working relationship, cats fulfil their work obligations entirely to their satisfaction.

Long-term residents of animal shelters will have an organized hierarchy of who sits and eats where and also who does what. A long-term study of cats in one shelter found that one individual cat, over the many years of her healthy life, took on the role of settling newcomers. The Settler cat greeted new inmates, many of whom were of course being relieved from otherwise horrible situations and were terrified of now being surrounded by strange cats. The Settler showed them where to eat, sit and sleep and often coaxed them out to the general play and mingle area. The Settler had made her position separate to the prevalent and ever-changing cat hierarchical structure, and this enabled her to fulfil her important role. Cat culture is varied and adaptive — not even territory rules are forever definite.

Cats are highly pragmatic and capable of rapid readjustment. Those abilities are often in high demand in the workplace. Other roles taken up by cats in shelters include 'head of security', ensuring all cats are behaving within generally acceptable lines, and 'greeter in chief', being the first cat to welcome any human visitors. Though cats do sleep a lot, up to sixteen hours a day, their jobs keep them busy, and they are not at all averse to hard work.

Consider the famous Dewey, whose story is delightfully told in the bestselling book, *Dewey: The small-town library cat who touched the world* by Vicki Myron. Dewey, who appeared one day in the library's return chute, had to calm down stressed children, keep the shelves clear of rodents, be welcoming and lovely to the lonely, recommend books to others, and ensure the staff were nice to each other.

Dewey was busy enough, but Felix the North Country British Railway cat, while being appointed senior pest controller by the TransPennine Express, also had people-calming duties. Kate Moore's *Felix the Railway Cat* recounts him taking on many other duties including accompanying each station supervisor on their daily rounds and supervising them.

Railway stations everywhere attract and benefit from cats, and often the human management is astute enough to appreciate them. None more so than the boss of Japan's Wakayama Electric Railway, whose cat, Tama, was promoted to senior station master at Kishi station. Tama was so appealing to visitors that an entire train was rebranded around her, and now her trainees are station masters at several other stops on the line.

You will find cats in many bookstores, generally keeping an eye on the place. Cats and books always seem to go together. T.S. Eliot put it this way: 'Books. Cats. Life is good.' The calmness of reading attracts the kind of people cats can be comfortable with. Jason Diamond writes in the Literary Hub, 'I can say without any doubt that bookstore cats represent the apex of domesticated pets. If a bookstore is so fortunate as to have a cat on the premises during operating hours, you can bet that feline is co-owner, manager, security and the abiding conscience of the place.'

Cats can intrigue and calm a child in the children's section, recommend the book you have taken down from the shelf and are reading, run up the ladders to point out a particular book for you, then patrol the tops of the cases to keep rodents away. Some cats have been known to leap onto customers' backs from this position, as a quicker way of getting back to floor level. However, other than this somewhat alarming practice, cats generally add to the normally calm nature of bookstores.

Even bookstores in frenetic areas like Los Angeles' Venice Beach can have a calming cat — which of course will make you want to stay longer. Then buy more books.

Cats are regular managers of pubs. There are books about this, though there are even for the most diligent of cats rather a lot of tempting distractions. Of course, cats should never touch alcohol, but some do.

Cats are extremely quick learners and once they have been fed by one diner, they know they are entitled to this kind of food and if the kitchen is good, they may find themselves neglecting mice altogether in favour of gourmet treats. Humans go to pubs in search of company as well as food and drink, and a warm, friendly cat provides a great deal of comfort; indeed, they can often be a reason for people to visit the pub in the first place. There's no easier way to start a conversation with a stranger than talking about the pub's resident cat. Cats of course know this — part of the responsibility involved in being a pub cat is taking care of deserving customers, checking the chairs for comfort and approving the food. Kind pub goers and owners have been known to notice how cats in their declining years become less interested in making new friends and fonder of very specific places to sleep. Beware the reaction of locals should you seek to turf a cat off the last remaining seat in the pub. That will be the cat's place, not yours.

There are hundreds of thousands of cats engaged by humans in the hospitality industry. Cat cafés, where you can go and be petted by one while you have your coffee, are appearing all over the world. They are marvellous places — the cat café in Melbourne, which has been up and running for nearly ten years, recruits its staff from shelters and advertises 'We have several adorable resident cats in a calm and relaxing environment where you can let your inner crazy cat person out!'

At time of writing there were sixteen cat cafés in business across Australia and five in New Zealand, and many of them offer an adoption service. For the cats. A few years ago, *Petful* magazine reported over 70 cat cafés spread across the United States and the wonderful website Meow Around lists about twenty in Canada. London's Lady Dinah's Cat Emporium states that it is the oldest one and charges per entry. Their website has particular rules and notes the sensibly evolved way you should interact with the cats, and for the initiated there is useful information there.

Official cat cafés are hundreds of years behind the unofficial ones. There is unlikely to be a small community in Great Britain or Ireland without at least one hospitality establishment supervised by a cat. It is also good to see that nowadays cats' experience has been put to good use when designing their holiday accommodation. The days of the 'cat motel' seem to be running out, with Britain leading the way with luxury hotels exclusively for cats, with rates at around £20 per night.

Cats are very clear about their preferences for friends, seating and food. Preferences for friends don't change, providing they behave themselves, and even a few minor errors of judgment are tolerated. It is cats' consistency in matters of friendship and companionship that helps them maintain the culture of a pub, a bookstore, a library or anywhere else cats work and people congregate — and that includes the political sphere.

Jacinda Ardern, New Zealand's youngest and most popular prime minister, was photographed being watched over by her cat, Paddles. 'I love this photo! No wonder your mummy won,' was the comment from one enthusiastic supporter.

Larry, who at time of writing has been the chief mouser and more besides at London's 10 Downing Street for over ten years, has seen off two Tory prime ministers and was known to enjoy Mr Cameron's lap, and is working even with Boris Johnson. Larry, however, drew the line at Donald Trump and chose to sleep under his car during his visit to number 10. Larry's playfulness, calmness and irreverence to pomp will have done much to maintain the general equilibrium of number 10.

President Bill Clinton's cat, Socks — who, like Larry, was once a stray — came under scrutiny from a Republican party member who wanted to know why the taxpayer had to pay for all of Socks' letters being mailed from the White House. Socks' letters were themselves the subject of a book by Hillary Clinton (and the royalties were donated). Socks answered just about every letter he received and also found time to supervise the children's section of the White House website. The good-natured warmth that Socks shared with children was so prolific that he had to organize a whole team of people to help him do it all, and Hillary's book underscored just how good a job Socks did in teaching the art of letter-writing to American children.

Canada's three-term Prime Minister Stephen Harper was maintained by a posse of animals while in office, and his cat Stanley — who came from the Ottawa Humane Society — was given his name by a vote involving over 11,000 people. While Stanley's name is shared with the cup given to the winner of the national hockey championship, Stanley was never known to be interested in hockey. Like some cats, he seems to have decided that his job was playing around. Anything seemed fun that did not include chasing mice. Cute-looking, and because Stephen's wife Laureen was a very active member of the Ottawa Humane society, Stanley would have been a poster boy for cat adoption.

Churchill's wartime cat, Nelson, had quite a lot of jobs to do, including being the prime ministerial hot water bottle, confidant, food taster and sometime companion when he chose to wander into cabinet meetings. More importantly, though, Nelson's pugnacious and fearless nature may well have been encouraging to Churchill himself. Nelson once chased a large dog away from London's Admiralty buildings and forced his predecessor as chief mouser right out the door of 10 Downing Street.

While Nelson may have been instrumental in keeping Churchill agitated and pugilistic, cats are now increasingly employed as therapy animals. Denver Airport has its own squad of cats that will calm you down and help you get your perspective back. Generally, cats just being themselves make excellent therapy animals. Consider the delightful English lass whose confidence and social skills were positively developed after the arrival of Thula the Maine Coon. As well as being gentle and large and unusually water loving, Maine Coons are highly communicative with a veritable array of chatty noises. For Iris Halmshaw, from the British Midlands, life with autism threatened to be somewhat lonely and difficult. Thula kept her company, chatting away, which encouraged Iris to speak and feel that she was sharing life. Iris, like some other children with autism, strongly disliked water but Thula's obvious enjoyment of it encouraged both bathing and swimming. Thula's constant companionship to Iris is well recorded in the book *Iris Grace* written by her mother, Arabella Carter-Johnson.

A cat therapy room in Adelaide described one of their therapy cats thus: 'Puck wants little more in life than to cuddle and be cuddled. Oh yes and food. Plenty of food. All food is good food.'

None of which is remotely unusual for a cat. But that's probably the point. The Adelaide business makes clear that their cats are actually trained and can cope with more than the cats you will find in cat cafés. Yet it is a cat's fundamental sociability and ability to determine on their own terms the job that needs doing which makes them such wonderful therapy animals, particularly for the frail and young, as cats are clearly a gentler choice than dogs or horses.

Sometimes, as was largely the case with Winston Churchill's cat Nelson, a cat's job is about helping you do yours. Morale in offices is much higher when cats are present. If you work from home, the company a cat will provide you — even if you know they are just gravitating towards your warm computer   can soothe anxiety and help concentration and your own productivity. Until they feel hungry. Cats perform a variety of other jobs, including advertising products for humans, and babysitting other cats and human children. Cats can also adopt other animals' young when they find them abandoned. Many museums and places of worship have feline tour guides to ensure that you gain the most from your visit. Cats have a natural tendency to want to navigate for humans. They are much better at it than us and most cats have on at least a few occasions walked their humans to and from the bedroom and the bathroom. And the kitchen.

Chicago's Tree House Humane Society's Cats at Work program transitions feral cats with a highly insecure future into fed, watered and cared-for hunters. The program does not seek to domesticate feral cats, but rather makes their lives better and gives them useful jobs dealing with rodents. For years now, the program has been placing several cats a week into these roles.

As well as protecting ordinary buildings from rodents, cats are in charge of pest eradication in many important museums and galleries, including the Hermitage Museum in Saint Petersburg, Russia, where for hundreds of years over 60 cats have safeguarded the priceless collections. Cats are also employed to keep large factory areas clear of mice, and no European farmyard is complete without at least one guard cat.

12

Cats in charge

I was introduced by a literary agent to Earl, who inhabited a large apartment in Manhattan. The agent had lent me her apartment for a week or so, and Earl was part of the deal. I was of course warned that 'Earl' was not the English 'milord' type, but rather the type of Earl you might meet at a diner in backcountry banjo land. The agent was quite right: Earl was missing an ear, had various battle scars (how he got them in an eighth-floor apartment I don't know) and looked tough — and he knew it. Having walked me around the apartment, returning twice to his food bowl and supplies, and making very sure that I knew where the fridge was, Earl returned me to an armchair and almost forced me into it, then sat on me for the rest of the week. Earl had taken advantage of the new person in the apartment and had managed it all perfectly well.

Stories of cats vomiting on temporarily unpopular people's beds, shredding their nice new tops, and pushing food they don't like into the dog's bowl are common enough. YouTube is replete with videos of cunning and naughty cats, but they are generally not being evil. Just trying to set the world right.

The editor of this book reports that when she was around thirteen years old, her brother, Michael, brought home a stray kitten from school, having saved it from some boys who were bullying it in the playground. The family named the cat Spook, and lavished attention on him. A few years later, Michael was talking to a female friend in the lounge room of the family's home — and decidedly not paying attention to Spook. This was of course most displeasing to the cat. Taking note of where Michael's attentions lay, Spook decided to take action ... by quietly reversing and peeing all over the legs of the poor girl. Needless to say, he got Michael's attention.

Sarah used to hide in my car, somehow getting in unnoticed before we drove off and staying perfectly hidden and quiet for a while, before leaping onto the passenger seat, whether or not there was a passenger there, and almost cackling aloud at the near accident-causing mayhem she created. She clearly thought that the idea of driving off without her was so unfathomable that she was never going to allow it.

My mother, Pamela, spent many of her last years with a little white, almost pink-eyed cat called Rosie. She looked sweet and lovely, and very fluffy as well. Rosie loved Pam but positively disliked every other human. All she ever wanted from humans came from Pam and, as far as she was concerned, all other people were just annoying. Normally shy of me, Rosie took up her position underneath the sofa whenever I visited. After what Rosie considered was a long enough visit, at least ten minutes, she started yowling. Apparently, she never did this when I wasn't around so — as Rosie intended — visits were kept short.

13

Cat toys

A superficial look suggests that cats put an exceptional amount of time and energy into making themselves comfortable. Compared to dogs, most of whom seem to be happy enough flopping down anywhere near you, cats are indeed particular. Fussy, some might say. But if you work out all the time you spend ensuring that your home and you are comfortable, warm, dry, well presented and safe, then the cat's efforts are comparable. Like you, cats are busy and have energy to burn.

Now that there is mounting pressure to make us keep cats indoors all the time, the list of what they need for full comfort has grown to include anything that can replicate the stimulation a hunting territory provides. If your cat cannot go out and climb trees, visit the neighbours, have a squabble with the cat over the road, threaten birds, terrorize mice and meet random new human admirers, what is a cat to do with all that energy? For many households, toys are the answer — ones your cat can play with on their own and ones that you will need to play along with.

Karen, a once feral cat, really didn't think much of the humans who were feeding her. They were good for a dinner and kept a warm house to sleep in, but they were dull compared to the wildlife. That was until I came home with a laser pointer. The guy at the pet shop said that they were the best thing about having cats. Operating like a torch and casting a pattern wherever pointed, the laser light can be moved anywhere you want. Karen chased it at attack pace across the house for days on end, until it was the humans who got tired, not her. A cat's ability to play and put themselves right into the moment is worth noting. When I was holding the laser light, Karen totally ignored me and instantly leapt upon the pattern. However, when I hid myself and landed the pattern near her Karen ignored it. The second I came into vision Karen then ignored me and set off after the pattern. Like it or not, I was part of the game and the game involved being a super-fast hunter who was far too busy to pay attention to the likes of me. Once the laser game had been established Karen seemed to want to spend much more time indoors, as if she could finally see a reason for sharing space with humans.

As well as the many cat toys you can make or buy to play with together, there is a huge variety of toys on offer that cats can play with alone. The online reviews are telling. Some owners think a particular toy is the best thing ever for their cat, while others think the same one might be a dangerous waste of space. Yes, cats are personal and have their own tastes. They can change, too; even Karen eventually got bored with the laser pointer. And any toy that is safe is predictable — and anything that becomes too predictable will after a while cease being of interest to the cat. Wise owners rotate the toys so the cat can be kept happy without spending a small fortune.

A good thing to think about when purchasing a cat's toy is where your cat will focus her eyes. Watch any cat getting ready for the

pounce and their eyes get a lot bigger, letting in light. If this happens occasionally with any toy, you know your cat is convinced. The more relaxed a cat is, the more their eyes seem half closed — so if playing with her toy causes the eyes to dilate you know she is getting ready to pounce. Food toys can do this — where the cat must find and either paw, claw, dig, scoop or tongue out their food. But I have noticed that any toy that's more than one-and-a-half times a cat's size is a bit too much for a cat to focus upon and enjoy.

Catnip filled and flavoured toys are among the best sellers. One popular version is a package of plastic ping pong-sized balls, some of which rattle as they roll across the floor. When infused or filled

with catnip they are often irresistible and will end up in every nook and cranny possible. Some reviewers complain that the balls crack and create a choking hazard, so you need to be vigilant. Jen, a reviewer on Amazon wrote, 'Foster cat loved these so much she busted in into the box in the middle of the night. They were a big hit. She slowly murdered them all.' Some cats put their little flavoured toys in their food box and carry them around in their mouths when they can. Accordingly, they never last long. An advantage of toys like this is that even kittens will play with them without you being there. When you first move or throw the toys, the kittens will quickly realize that the toys are mobile and some will even compete to drive them all behind the fridge.

A moving plush fish is a very popular toy; they have a motion sensor and start wriggling when the cat approaches. They are recharged via a USB port, and some come with a catnip-filled pouch and a removable cover. Reviews suggest that cats squabble over who has rights to it at what times, and that it's a rare thing to find 'a toy my cat doesn't get bored with within a day'. Melissa, an Amazon reviewer, reported that 'All three cats looked at me like they wanted to smack me for buying such a stupid item.' Another reviewer reported the opposite: 'My three cats have been playing with it almost non-stop except when I have to take it away to charge it.'

Toys with a static base that spin or roll around, especially those with balls on several levels, can intrigue, and some can be played with alone or in a cat team. Sun Fish wrote this Amazon review: 'I have a feral cat that took me five years to catch and tame. She *loves this toy*. I'd even say she is obsessed with it.' Another reviewer commented, 'We have seven cats. Only one showed any interest.'

Toys where a cat can use its paw to rotate a wheel, wands with feathers, mice or just fabric at the end are all popular. So too are all kinds of shapes, from bananas to pelicans stuffed with catnip; and especially popular are those that squeak like a bird, as well as toys that keep moving of their own accord.

Cats will determine what their toys are, whether you issue them or not, and their choices include boxes, saucepans, newspapers, little balls and anything that can be batted around, and particularly items that are responsive to light. Remember, though, play is surrogate hunting and most toys will end up being destroyed and potentially eaten. You can grow catnip indoors and outdoors, and although some cats are allergic to it most adore it, so it can be used to make anything more appealing; placed on the floor, it may well be rolled all over.

The Humane Society of the United States reports that 'Catnip sensitivity is hereditary — an estimated 50 per cent of cats have no reaction'. A cat's high can last for as long as ten minutes but generally kittens under six months old are not so affected by the volatile oil found in the stems and leaves of catnip.

As well as toys, other indoor cat paraphernalia can (perhaps should) include a scratching area (whether or not the cat is declawed). If your windowsill is not big enough for the cat there are contraptions you can attach for him to lie on and look outdoors. Becoming more popular are mini cat houses, which provide an enclosed safe space, and also end up being used as a place to hide toys. Be careful with some of the products that combine some kind of toy, a scratching post and a bed. They may well be very space efficient and a potentially shrewd buy, but cats like to roam and explore and will have their own opinions. Micrea wrote on Amazon: 'My cat hated it but my mum's cat loves it … my cat was a stray … he doesn't like to put himself in situations where he cannot escape'. If you are looking for a safe space for your cat, consider providing simple things that they can choose to be their safe spot. Like toys, all things a cat truly appreciates are chosen by him regardless of your help.

14

Fighting and military strategy

I am as vigilant as a cat to steal cream.

Shakespeare's Henry IV Part 1

Cat lovers are not always comfortable discussing these martial aspects of their feline friends. Somehow the dichotomy of the soft, furry, affectionate, cuddle-loving lap cat also being a violent, murderous hunter and fighter is hard to bear.

Feline martial prowess is fundamental to who they are and some of the tactics employed are quite endearing — and many are used on you, whether you know it or not.

If your cat is free to roam or has some outside area to call her own, you are less likely to see some of these traits than if she were housebound. The longer she is housebound the scarier 'the outside' will become for her and you will see all her personality traits. Common to house and outdoor cats is a constant alertness to danger and opportunity when awake. When your cat is very tense — for example, when another animal is present — be aware that your cat is never that far away from a wild state and can lash out.

Most of the world's military forces are long on parades, strutting and posing and being as intimidating as possible. Cats do some of this too. There are not many cats who have not delivered a paw swat or two to just about everything that moves around them. Normally the claws are retracted but the message is clear: 'Don't mess with me, I can keep order around here because actually I can be fast and tough. Grumpy too, so behave yourself.'

If you consider, just for a moment, the company that cats keep — that's people like us — it is not surprising that that they have not let go of their martial skills. For a start, humans fight among themselves all the time. It seems to be the done thing. Humans are unreliable feeders and benefactors, and most cats will have seen or heard of others ending up, when they are lucky, in shelters. Your cat may trust you, but he probably has good reason not to fully trust humans, so he needs to keep his primal skills attuned.

There is also the problem of too many other cats as, despite all the evidence and needs and benefits, some humans don't bother with having cats neutered and there are struggles for territory, which can turn nasty. Cat fights lead to a high proportion of all visits to the vet. If your cat is often outside it's a tough world out there. She is not scratching your sofa to pieces just so she can claw at mice or whizz up trees; paws are weapons.

One of the greatest experts on military strategy, Carl von Clausewitz, has been quoted as seeing war as 'Primordial violence, hatred and enmity, which are to be regarded as a blind natural force; of the play of chance and probability within which the creative spirit is free to roam.' Clausewitz was not writing about cats, but much of this is relevant. 'Primordial violence', known as a 'blind natural force', can be seen and sensed in the brief intense fury of a typical cat fight. Cats will leap upon each other with more venom and hatred than any immediate set of circumstances we can imagine could possibly engender. Ears and the striking paws are often the main targets, and the noisy fight is normally very quickly over.

What is not relevant from Clausewitz is 'hatred and enmity'. Certainly, that exists in the immediate moments around the fight, but cats don't often bear grudges and it is not uncommon to see cats quickly repair friendships. 'The play of chance and probability' is a neat way of defining a cat's great opportunistic abilities. As you know, cats do set themselves goals, they do strategize and think long and hard. The next time you see your cat with eyes half closed seemingly contemplating the world, she could be thinking about strategy. Cats are also great tactical opportunists and can pounce upon any unsuspecting opportunity as much for the glee of it as for any purpose. If you have left a piece of fish on the kitchen counter there is a clear chance for the cat, and if you are out if the room there is a good probability that she will capture it.

As well as being truly alive and creative in the moment, a cat's planning can also be remarkable. Where a cat chooses to eat, sleep and sit, which cats to make friends with, and how and when to check the territory can all be driven by offensive and defensive strategies. If your house has stairs a cat will enjoy the safety of being in a higher position that no other cat can assail without being seen.

A martial and a general life strategy is to change the agenda. If a mouse slips down a hole that the cat 'couldn't really be bothered' to stalk again you will see that the cat, far from giving up the chase, will all of a sudden find an absorbing new interest. Perhaps checking out a sunny spot not so far away. Cats lose interest in fights very quickly, as there is always something more interesting to look at.

When fighting, changing the agenda may not always work, especially if the antagonist seems to be very focused. Now that you have noticed that your fish has gone missing you could well be the antagonist seeking to have a gentle word while perhaps waving the delicately picked bone at the cat.

It's going to be hard for the cat to change the agenda here. Another tactic is used. It's one of his favourites: diplomacy. Quite likely your cat will rush towards you with much louder purrs and demonstrably greater affection than he has shown in weeks. 'Thank you, thank you for thoughtfully leaving that fish ready for me; that was so kind of you. You really are a lovely person. Oh, I don't need the bone but thank you very much for reminding me.' He will have found a way to clamber onto you and your heart will have melted. He has diplomatically suggested that you prepared the fish for him and, of course, being a true cat lover, you are not about to disabuse him of this perspective.

But what if you are made of sterner stuff? The 'change the agenda' tactic can be used in different ways. Jumping upon forbidden tables or up curtains will achieve the distraction required. Now if you are of a particularly stubborn disposition and, after calm has been restored, insist on talking about the fish, your cat will revert to two other tactics. The first of these is to seek to change your values. Expect a long quizzical look that says, 'You are waving a fish bone at a cat climbing a curtain; isn't it time you got a hold of yourself? Just how ridiculous are you?'

He will have a point.

The second approach is a bare-faced lie: 'What are you talking about? You know I am not allowed on the kitchen counter so it couldn't have been anything to do with me, could it?' With the second tactic, playful or otherwise, a cat will often use distraction techniques. The default position is often that 'I am too cute, furry and cuddly to do anything other than play with, and if you are human, cuddle and feed me'.

That doesn't work with other cats, but it might trick a cat-hearted dog or two. The cat's fundamental strategic aim is to make the antagonist see something different to what is there and to break the antagonist's concentration. In human military schools, the Trojan Horse is a great example of distraction. A cat seeking to avoid a pouncing fight can quite often, if you watch carefully, be seen to suddenly pounce upon prey. For all cats, especially the street-fighting kind, an immediate meal is much more interesting than a street fight and the adversary will come over to have a look, at which time the crafty cat has left — and of course there was no prey to be had. If a Trojan Horse technique cannot be used, the cat will move to optical illusion and run around in zig zags and leap so quickly that not even another cat will be sure where the other one is. Concentration is broken and the agenda changed back to whatever the cats were doing before the spat.

Tackling more difficult adversaries, including overly curious dogs, sometimes requires additional skills.

Bare-faced bluffing is standard in canine encounters. Human armies pretend to be bigger and more powerful than they are. So too do cats, who, for example, will crouch forward, raise their tail and bush up and march upon what are often bamboozled but much larger dogs. A complementary tactic is to outflank a chasing dog, moving to the side of the pursuit's direction and circling around or attacking from the side. Of course, dogs are generally more physically powerful than any cat. Head-to-head fights are inadvisable. The weapons at the cat's disposal include explosive speed over short distances, climbing ability, and electrically fast reflexes that can lead to a dog's face being swatted before the dog has worked out what's going on. Dogs can also be dealt with by one of the cat's favourite tactics. Stealth.

Your domestic cat is a little different to some of its big sisters and brothers. She will not come out well in a direct tussle with any substantial adversary who is prepared for battle. If conflict is inevitable and all other tactics are irrelevant, the cat will pounce or leap from totally unexpected places. Ponk likes to lurk on a windowsill, which somehow fits him though it's too small for the average snail. No bird, to their loss, has ever expected him to be there. A sheep rambling uninvited into her home's garden was surprised when Sarah dropped from a tree right onto her woolly back. A gently nosing dog will suddenly find a cat immediately in front of him or, worse still, bearing down fast on his side. Cats need to be driving the agenda to be successful (which might be why you always feel that they have the last word).

Cheyenne and Max

Stealth normally leads to ambush. Knowing her territory, a cat will have a thorough knowledge of the best places to launch an ambush from in defence, in capturing prey and at home in play. Sarah loved being cuddled on the family bed. The problem was that come bedtime humans pranced around the bedroom, changing clothes, popping in and out of the bathroom, drawing curtains, finding books and generally doing everything except what she wanted them to do, which was settle in or on the bed.

Sarah found a way of getting the attention she wanted. The bedroom was long and narrow and everyone moving around there had to navigate a narrow corner around the bed. You had to be careful, though, as a single cat's leg would shoot out at the critical moment, making you jump aside and the only place to go was onto the bed. Should I have ever doubted that cats have a sense of humour, this frequent but unpredictable tactic would have been more than enough proof, and I am sure her head would have been shaking with mirth. As soon as you were on the bed, Sarah very politely jumped up with a lick and a purr.

Another famous military strategist, Sun Tzu, is credited with saying 'Keep your friends close: your enemies closer' and cats are particularly adept at this. A cranky, hostile neighbour may quickly be overrun by a determined charm offensive, especially if done in tandem with another housemate cat — who can resist a pair of snuggling cats smiling at them from the doorstep? This strategy also works well with dogs who are not the naturally kind type; cats are very often smarter and convince the dogs that they need the cat's protection.

All good armies are constantly training, and cats train to fight in their litter and constantly practise with their friends. This can include you and your housemate and particularly children, and of course each other.

15

What your cat thinks of you

Food provider or issuer? Surrogate mother cat and dominant boss of the house? Boss of the garden? Rule breaker or maker? Amazing hunter or hopeless kitten? Playmate or treacherous lover? Yes, it's complicated. Cats don't think like humans and sometimes we are just plain incomprehensible to them.

A key to understanding this is that cats are consistent and when they see that we are not, they are perplexed. For example, one morning you might be quietly slipping a morsel or two to your cat while she sits on your lap at the breakfast table. Okay, so she had your bacon. She is now entitled to it. We will call her Karen. The next morning you are sharing breakfast with someone else and when Karen makes her move towards breakfast you put her down on the ground. For the cat, this is just confusing and outrageous.

'What,' Karen will ask, 'is going on?' Karen will look at your plate — oh, it's those funny carboard-type things that come from a packet. Maybe that's the problem, she thinks: he wants me to go and get some proper food. Karen then disappears, you finish breakfast and Karen arrives back with a mouse. You are feeling a bit guilty about turfing her off your lap earlier, so you make a big fuss of her and make 'you are a super hunter, clever cat, Karen' noises. Satisfied, she goes off to sleep. You remove the mouse.

Later, Karen wakes up, thinks you have eaten the mouse and goes off in search of another. It's not hard. If cats lived on mice alone, they would need to catch nearly one mouse for every waking hour, so Karen comes back quickly and finds you. You are talking with your new partner, who is not as keen on cats as you are, so you think you need to make a fuss. 'No no,' you say (you are a cat lover so you wouldn't be crass enough to shout — that would take weeks to recover from) and lift Karen up with the mouse still in her mouth, open the forbidden door and throw her out of it.

Now this will really take a lot of thinking about. Karen is completely confused. You have just rejected what it was you so wanted and obviously needed just one sleep ago. Further, you broke your own rule by opening the sliding door that you have previously (and obviously now) pretended you couldn't open any time she meowed at it to be let in. Heck, she even banged it with both front paws, but you still pretended it was impossible. What is going on? This really is all a bit much and requires a good long sleep to sort it out.

That evening you and your partner are alone again, and Karen, demanding a lap, finds you and yes — many cat lovers will do this accidentally — you let slip a little bit of your dinner while trying to distract your partner by pointing at the noisy coloured box. The only reasonable conclusion your cat can make at this time is that either your partner has bewitched you in some way or you have gone mad. As Karen personally selected you as a vital staff member, madness must be ruled out. Stalking your partner must begin. The only good thing about this partner is that she doesn't challenge you all the time, and in fact never looks at you at all. However, there must be something she is doing to stop you being fed extras and be thrown out of forbidden doors with rejected mice.

The first line of attack will be comprehensive sniffing. Is your partner involved with any other cats? Is your cat's territory in question? This thought will make a cat truly anxious. If you have a new live-in partner or even a regular visitor who will be bringing cat scent into your home, your cat will know and be worried. So, make sure your cat knows that she is far more important than any visitor and is not threatened. If your new partner is smart, they'll start issuing the food. Karen will know that you didn't hunt it yourself — she has seen you bringing in the kill wrapped in bright bags — but at least the interloper may have some use. After all this, Karen will probably be involved in other issues. It's busy being a cat. There is a lot to deal with, especially all those sounds, smells and emotions. But, however friendly Karen may be to all well-intentioned comers, you are the special one. Just about every cat has one person who is more important than anybody else. Yes, that makes that person (I am assuming it is you) the centre of life. It doesn't mean that any cat will automatically condone or approve of your actions; often far from it. But it does mean she will more quickly forgive and forget than she would any crimes from anyone else. Some cat behaviourists believe that the person in this focal position for the cat has taken over the role of their mother. Certainly, some feline maternal roles do come with this, and nurturing and caring are assumed. But most kittens are wrested from their mother after six weeks and cats aren't going to remember much about how their mum behaved. They will, though, remember the feeding, the feelings of security and even the games they started to play with mum and the rest of the litter, often starting after just two weeks alive. You most certainly will be expected to play games with her. But you are not Mum. You don't sound, smell or look like her; you just do a few of the vital things she did.

If you generally live alone, or with people who let you believe it, you probably are the boss of the house and Karen will believe it. She will see you lighting fires or making the heater work, turning on or off the coloured talking box. These will seem like boss-type actions. But the most important is giving right of access into the territory and never having to ask anyone for permission to enter. There is no banging on doors or pressing buzzers, let alone meowing or waving at the window.

16

Your cat
as your friend

Unlike many people in households, your cat specifically chose to live with you, and it will be wise to remember this. Most cats can feed themselves and if not will inveigle themselves into someone else's heart and home with impressive speed. Having no luggage to take with her (and often there is a cat door), make no mistake: your cat chooses to be with you. You might think it's all about the food, the admiration, the warm spaces, the safety of a known territory, and in part you will be right, but those are all replicable elsewhere. So, you are the chosen one. Which is surprising, as your cat thinks that you are a slob. Your cat thinks your manners are shocking.

First, your family's eating habits are only redeemed because the cat generally benefits from them. Eating for cats is a quiet, efficient, solitary process. Everything on the plate is normally eaten and anything left behind is not 'for later' — it's just unwanted and left to the ants. Humans, however, make a big song and dance around eating. They linger around half-empty plates, stop eating halfway through to do something with the talking box, and have long conversations with each other. They also guzzle vast amounts of liquid while eating. Cats eat quickly and normally drink at other times. Feeding, unless with young or some especially close feline friends, is solitary. It is always quick. This means that no other cats have much chance of stealing anything. Most cats are very clean when they eat. Humans leave mess everywhere. Well, some goes on the floor and a good tidy cat will do what she can to clean it up for you. As for what you eat, much of that is inexplicable, but your cat will not blame you for trying and will sniff everything she can of yours to try to understand its appeal. My childhood cat, Sarah, generally shook her foot at anything she considered inedible. But once she actually hissed at a pile of greens that had accidentally fallen into her plate. She thought that was just an insult.

After cats eat, they fastidiously wash themselves, leaving no food scents to attract rivals or predators or even fleas. Humans generally just go about their business, reeking of their last meal. Even worse, they sometimes don't wash their plates immediately. The times you may have your left your unclean plate out overnight resulted in your poor cat having no sleep while seeking to guard the house from the inevitable predators you were almost deliberately inviting in.

We won't be talking about humans' bathroom habits, which are at best inexplicable to a cat, but your lack of manners with other humans does require some perspective. For cats, the polite and proper thing to do when reacquainting yourself with others is a quick sniff, the appropriate status reflected in body language and very rarely any immediate sounds. Humans in any household either totally ignore each other, or shout or grunt, especially in the mornings, and can be all over each other in the evenings. Then the human concept that a single moment in conversation — a sentence — should only have one idea is also perplexing to cats. They are far

more sophisticated communicators, regularly conveying a lot in one instant. A softly swishing, lowered tail with one ear leaning forward and the other vertical with both eyes staring at you and a quiet meow says a lot, including 'It's lovely to see you, how nice, I am very happy about that. I am glad I am here at the centre of life. Yet I am very hungry, so please feed me now. In fact, I am so hungry that if you don't feed me there is a danger that there could be trouble. As you can see, I am trying to control this right now, but I won't manage that for long.'

One of the things that matters to your cat is that you are entirely unchallenging and uncompetitive. You cannot run very fast, you cannot dive down rabbit holes or whizz up trees, leap though the air and, at least in the cat's territory, you are hopeless at hiding. She is better at everything that matters. Yet you have clearly recognized this and go to great lengths to try to keep up with her. Judging by the number of bags you bring home you have clearly learnt hunting skills from her, albeit without much discrimination. As for her thoughts on all the inedible and uncomfortable things you bring home — well, they are probably unprintable.

You can also be annoying. Very. Cats' hearing is at least fourteen times better than yours, so when your turn up your speakers or your TV you are causing her potential distress, and you are certainly creating what she will sense as noise pollution. Just a few notes on the piano would have Sarah in attack mode, and seeing feet move at the pedals she would attack them as the cause of the problem. At times she would realize that I was attached to the feet, so she would then try to clamber into the piano through an impossibly small space. But she made it possible.

Cats generally do not bear grudges, but they seldom forget potential trouble spots. As Sarah was growing up, my piano playing declined from being just bad to being positively frightful. Sarah blamed the piano or whatever lurked inside it as the cause of the unacceptable racket. Coming home one day, I could not find her. But I heard her and traced her meowing to the piano's part of the room. This wasn't her normal 'Please come and find me as I cannot get out of this ridiculous place, I have parked myself in' meow. This set of meows I came to understand meant, 'I have been tricked by the thing in here, it's gone away but it's locked me in and that's unfair and outrageous and you are responsible.' It didn't seem possible to extricate Sarah, even though it must be possible; after all she had got in. But there was no space to reach her. My father had the idea of playing a few bars and that sound seemed to collect all Sarah's wits and she shot out of the tiny gap she had clambered through. Clearly, it was all the humans' fault.

The other musical instrument that tended to bemuse Sarah was my sister Alyss's flute. Undoubtedly, she was better with it than I was at the piano, but our mother once charitably described the noise she produced as akin to a demented owl's. Sarah thought one was obviously hiding inside the silver stick Alyss was blowing into and took to hovering around the end of it, ready to pounce the moment the owl blew out.

Humans on their own tend to turn on electronic noise, and in groups they get louder. A group of cats, even when not somnolent, is, apart from brief ferocious exceptions, quiet.

But despite being messy, uncouth and impolite and noisy, your cat loves you and overlooks your faults as all good and real friends do. In fact, you are probably the centre of his life. How can this be? You will know that he will be quite distressed when you are away for a longer period than normal and will be waiting near the door to pointedly ignore you upon your return. Once you have noticed that you have been ignored, he will make his loving feelings known.

The one thing cats really find annoying about humans is that they simply won't leave them alone. The disturbed, slightly troubled look that cats give when they are discovered in their safe, sleepy hiding place is generally misinterpreted. The cats are saying, 'Oh please go away — I know you love and need me, but I have sleeping to do.' But we think they are saying, 'Just look how cute I am. Pick me up now please.'

That cats have feelings for their humans that transcend appreciation for practical things is, I suspect to anyone reading this, completely obvious. It is extraordinary therefore that scientists need to study this and express surprise that, yes, cats do miss their humans and get stressed when they are not there. There is a lot of scientific research into cats, and we will see in the next chapter how useful, if at all, some of this is. The irony, which will be lost on those with monochromatic minds, is that cats are more sophisticated than anything that can be factually defined and that, of course, is one of the reasons why we find them appealing.

17

The scientific cat

Cats' very nature makes them a difficult subject for scientists, but cats conduct scientific experiments themselves. Many concerning you. Much loved by physics professors, Hooke's Law suggests that small changes to an elastic object are in ratio to the force making the changes, and once you have finished distorting an object it will return to its previous form. This theory is almost 400 years old but cats are still checking this. If you look carefully, you are likely to see your cat testing this around the home. The drapes or curtains in your living room can be probed by running up and down them. It's very rare that you see these fabrics piled up on the floor so the theory has some resonance. What about the glass jar on the counter? Push it this way? No change. How about that way? No change either; this Hooke guy must have been onto something. Will just try it this way. Oops, it smashed on the ground and here come the humans who have been ignoring me this morning so, though clearly flawed, Hooke has been helpful. Now let's apply some scientific research to another one of these human laws: gravity. That's the law that suggests that it's a natural force that causes things to fall towards the earth. Cats are deeply sceptical about this and frequently test it. The glass jar falling looked like it might have proven the point, but as the cat pushed it there is no proof there and as he can leap vertically upwards when required, the whole gravity theory is somewhat in doubt.

Scientific study requires close observation and analysis, which is one of the reasons you will always find your cat getting close to whatever she finds intriguing. Testing the strength of objects is a standard piece of feline research, with results that sometimes astonish even them. There is little that a determined cat cannot break down to miniscule parts.

If you are an inconstant kind of person a cat is unlikely to be interested in you. Despite thousands of years of exposure, we remain pretty weird creatures to them, so if you are behaving in unreliably eccentric ways, they are not going to waste their time on you. Part of a cat's research on you is to work out if you are consistent enough to bother with. After all, you can only be useful if you are managed properly.

Most people believe that the first decision a cat makes about any human is whether the human likes cats at all. But experience suggests that good manners are more important than anything else. You will find that what you see as a cat testing your patience may in fact be him seeing if you have kept your own standards up. Hiding in plain sight when you call him is a simple test. He wants to know how much effort you are going to put into finding him. How much you love him. He heard you perfectly well the first time — his hearing is significantly better than yours — but hearing you

keep on shouting for him might make him feel important. Another test for you is seeing if you notice that he moves the position of the food bowls. If in the evening the water bowl is to the right of his food bowl, see if they are the same way around in the morning. If you don't move them, he will assume that you haven't noticed and will conduct an additional test of your observational skills, and this time combine it with an assessment of your olfactory competencies. A test much favoured by cats who spend time outdoors is playing hide the mouse. Can you find it before the ants (or worse) do? A much-loved scientific experiment is checking on the theory of gravity. After all, cats can leap vertically, given enough stimulus, so the theory will need periodic testing. Items on a kitchen bench that can be moved to its edge offer prime opportunities for empirical research — humans will rapidly become very interested in the process and can take notes and comment as the theory of gravity is seen to be proven.

Human research into cat behaviour recently produced a study titled 'The "Feline Five": An exploration of personality in pet cats (*Felis catus*)', which identified five prevalent behavioural types: extraversion, neuroticism, agreeableness, dominance and impulsiveness. Yes, I know your cat probably demonstrates a lot of all of these. The study noted:

> Neuroticism reflects strongest levels of traits, such as insecure, anxious, fearful of people, suspicious and shy; dominance reflects bullying, dominant and aggressive to other cats; impulsiveness reflects impulsive, erratic and reckless; and agreeableness reflects affectionate, friendly to people and gentle. However, our fifth factor extraversion also revealed traits normally associated with self-control in Scottish wildcats including decisive, aimless, persevering and quitting.[1]

We will look at these from the cat's perspective.

Neuroticism

Not all cats are automatically good as pets and there are studies which suggest that cats, who can manage quite well without you thank you, can either be disturbed by all the fuss and attention you are providing or pick up on your own styles of living. So, if you think your cat is neurotic you should have a good look at your own behaviour.

Science Alert looked at a study of over 3000 cat owners by Lauren Finka, an animal welfare researcher in Nottingham. 'High owner neuroticism was linked with cats cited as having behavioural problems, which could be evidenced by aggression, anxiety or fear, or stress related behaviours ...' The research also showed that 'cat owners who scored higher on extroversion were more likely to have animals that themselves enjoyed more freedom outside, while participants who came across as agreeable reported being more satisfied with their (perhaps more agreeable) felines'.[2]

Cats don't necessarily interpret human behaviour as we do. For example, if you see someone feeding a cat from their plate at the table saying in a kind, gentle voice 'Just this once' the cat won't understand the restriction. She will reasonably assume that this is now a new way of feeding that she is entitled to. So, when she jumps up the next time and is picked up and put down and growled at, or worse, she will be terribly upset. You are behaving in an unkind, irrational manner. You are like that whenever you go away for a few days, no matter who is cat-sitting. Yes, cats can and do look after themselves but when they are bonded to you and you become inconsistent it will make them cautious, even nervous, and this is often how cats become neurotic and suspicious. As for 'anxious and fearful', there will be reasons you will have to deduce in order to solve the problem of why — nobody wants their cat to be stressed. Signs of fear and anxiety in your cat include causing

damage, trying to get out of the house more, even trembling and scratching the floor. Often the solution, if it is not something that a vet points out to you, is spending a lot of time and care with your cat. Coriander, a rescue cat, could not be calmed when she first moved into my home. Her companion, Bandicoot, who came from the same shelter, settled in immediately. But for Coriander, yet another home was going to be difficult. She spent most evenings on my lap where she did settle, but always looked miserable when I went to work. It couldn't go on, so I decided to spend a week at home away from the office, which would hopefully settle her. We discussed this at home and agreed it was the right thing to do. However, once that decision was made, towards the end of the preceding week Coriander brightened up, became calmer and more settled, and we spent many happy years together. I don't believe Coriander's change was coincidental; I suspect she sensed that her welfare was of major concern for the household and that was sufficient to let her know she was in a safe forever home.

Dominance

The second characteristic identified in the research was dominance. For the most part, two or more cats living together will get along. Think of them like young teenaged boys. There will be posturing and posing and bluster of all kinds, food pilfering, the occasional squabble and lots of fun and games. The bluster includes face-offs and chases and there will just occasionally be brief but terrifyingly noisy fights. As cats get a little older, say, three or four years, males' interest in females reaches a competitive fever pitch, and like lions in a pride there are fights for the prime position. Yes, cats can bully other cats, and yes you should intervene to make sure that you, as possibly the most important mammal around, bestow your status upon the bullied one. This can give reassurance to the cat that needs it most and creates a little, and probably temporary, distortion in the social order, which gives time for the bully cat or cats to attend to something else — which hopefully will not be your neighbour's Pekingese. Cats' behaviour in this regard is no different to many other mammals. Sometimes your cat may appear to be aggressive with you or another cat for no obvious reason. It's probably just because you are in the way. You will understand that cats are intensely emotional creatures. Unlike some humans they cannot compartmentalize their feelings. So, if there is fighting in the air, noises or invaders outside, the cat will act immediately and, as you are there, it will also, naturally, be your problem.

Fighting, bullying and caterwauling are easy to record and even film, count and draw scientific conclusions about. But nearly all the time cats are not being dominant and aggressive or seeking to mate. They are being far more engaging, so it's a mistake to try to understand cats by focusing too much on this behaviour.

So how about the next item listed in the study: impulsiveness?

Impulsiveness

The *Shorter Oxford English Dictionary* includes being swayed by emotion in its definition of impulsiveness. Humans describe each other as impulsive if they don't do things the same way, and describing someone thus is less than flattering. But cats are ruled by a sometimes conflicting hierarchy of emotions. The emotion that is currently at the top of the hierarchy will determine the cat's immediate actions. So, as can often be the case, if your cat feels an overwhelming sense of love for you and leaps into your arms, he is being no more impulsive than he might be the next day, when he sees and ignores you as he is hunting at the time and you are in the way. Both responses are entirely consistent with what being a cat is all about. Cats may appear to be erratic, but they are consistently following their compass.

If someone calls a cat reckless, they are possibly relying upon a profoundly flawed analysis. What would your behaviour be like if your skills proportionally matched a healthy cat? You could probably leap over 70-metre (230-foot) distances, vertically jump 10 metres (33 feet) high, hear and smell fourteen times better than you do and land securely when dropping from great heights. If you had those skills and used them in front of sentient beings who didn't, they might consider you to be the reckless one.

Agreeableness

In the same way that neurotic people house neurotic cats, disagreeable cats can be found in predictable places. So, the reverse is probably true. Cats are not always complicated; once their food, shelter, warmth, security, mental and physical stimulus requirements along with the necessity for lots of loving attention have all been met, a cat will be happy. Providing, of course, you adjust for her changing palate, needs for peace and privacy, and admire and leave her alone enough. If you are doing all these things and your cat is still disagreeable you should look at health and territorial concerns.

Agreeable or otherwise, cats will always project some of their key human ally's characteristics. All cats have one person they believe is the leader of their household, or who they think is in most need of them, and they will behave like them when it suits. So, the proverbial hissing witch's cat or grumpy old man's bossy cat, or teenage girl's pretty cat are all taking their characteristics from their key human.

18

Our ways with cats

Putting constraints on a cat is a test of anyone's character, no more so for some than putting their cat on a leash.

If yours is a house cat and spends much time chattering away at the windowsill, he may well feel that he owns the whole street and will want to get out there. Having him on a leash, you can at least do this safely. Leashes are becoming much more popular and, apart from the risk of attack from dogs wandering free, it's a much safer way for your cat to see the world. There is a low risk of being run over (which for free-ranging cats is the single most common form of premature death) and your cat, and you, can get some good bonding exercise together. This is also a safe approach for potential prey, and for the cat at least it will be mentally stimulating. Though not appropriate for every cat, including those that can be easily scared, doing this will improve many housebound cat's lives, so expect to see much more of this as it's becoming more popular. When your cat is stimulated either by running free outside or going out with you (albeit on a leash) you will find that any aggression, boredom or stress he was displaying at home is likely to be quickly mitigated.

Walking your cat on a leash requires a different approach to dog walking, so as well as checking that all vaccinations are up to date and that you have a proper harness and leash, get some professional advice. There are plenty of informative websites and your vet is likely to have some valuable views, too. It can take a while. I know an illustrator in Perth who reckons it took almost a year to properly train her older cat, and even then, she just walks him in the very early hours. So ideally start when your cat is young — it will be quicker — and be patient and persistent and don't expect her to always be happy about the idea.

When you understand the nature of your cat and what they like and are likely to do, you will find that the cat's confidence in you, and herself, will increasingly grow. Karen, like other cats, was happy having me in the garden while she was out prowling. I was someone to show off to and a source of safety. Though of course she was always far too busy doing important things to overtly acknowledge my presence. I made a point of not looking at Karen when I returned to the house, and being very noisy about it. Sure enough, she quickly followed me in and was always a happy cat at the time. Learning your cat's foibles is a lifelong exercise but the more you can accommodate these the happier she will be. No cats are alike, and they even expect different treatment from different people. There is a story of how a cat transferred her attentions to her owner's new boyfriend, and it took the owner a while to figure out that the cat preferred the boyfriend's rough and tumble play style to the more delicate touch she was used to. Some people believe that there are cats who always favour males and others who always prefer females. This has not been my experience, but it's

worth taking a note of what your cat enjoys doing with members of the opposite sex.

Often, you gain your cat's trust by doing the obvious things before she asks, like keeping to meal times, chasing a visiting cat from the garden, and so forth. If you have held your cat in an otherwise precarious position since she was very little, she is going to enjoy big physical adventures with you. A cat's trust is something you must earn, and the rewards are unforgettable. When Bandicoot and Coriander were young, I sensed a big storm was coming in. They, of course, already knew something bad was about to happen and were huddled next to each underneath a garden bench. I battened down the house, scooped them up and had them playing

with me on the bed, which was their favourite thing. Their joint look of relief, almost bliss, is permanently in my memory.

It's important to encourage kittens in their adventures — the world is a big, fascinating and scary place. So, if she is attempting something brave and she knows that you are there, never encourage and applaud. Whatever you do, do not laugh at any failures or for that matter laugh at a cat at all. It's the height of rudeness.

Robert Heinlein, the science fiction writer, once said that 'if you want to know a man observe how he treats a cat'. Both distorting and using this insight has been a ploy of movie makers. The James Bond villain Blofeld has a pretty white Persian alongside him. The opening scene of *The Godfather* has Vito Corleone stroking his

Cheyenne dozing

grey tabby, again disguising the character's murderous nature. J.K. Rowling's tabby Mrs Norris is an ideal skulking alter ego to her miserable Filch, with each illuminating the other's character. How you treat your cats will say much about you and there are high standards to follow — cats make exemplary mothers and know what 'looking after' means. Male cats generally have nothing to do their young except in their roles as dominant cats within their communities, so if you look at a group of strays or feral cats you may find that 'he' steps in to comfort a stressed kitten or break up a fight, but they generally have no interest. Some of the big cats are known to eat other cats' offspring, so male cats are probably programmed with the lowest possible standards.

In general, humans tend to bother cats rather more than they seem to like. Yes, some cats want to be permanently glued to you. Many others like being around you and that is sufficient interaction. The cat wants to choose when it's play and cuddle time; at other times it can be sufficient to gently acknowledge her presence, like two respectful men nodding silently as they pass in the street. Consider it from the cat's point of view. You are noisy, smelly, very big, probably clumsy and at times painfully demanding. It's not that the cat doesn't think you have some cuteness and are even lovable, but there is much going on in a cat's life, and you are just one of many parts. So, leave your cat alone a little more. Kittens seem to prefer more attention, and a colleague Alice's kittens thrived during a Covid lockdown and were totally happy to have both humans at home full-time for weeks on end.

Michel de Montaigne observed that 'When I play with my cat, who knows if I am not more of a pastime to her than she is to me?' Part of the joy of cats is their independence from you. Like true lovers, they choose to be with you every single time. Unlike dogs, they will survive and maybe even flourish without you. I have found that when there are two well-bonded cats in a household, they together contextualize their relationship with humans. They will need even

Totoro by the fire

less of you, but you are more likely to be seen as a fellow playmate as well as a food provider.

Heinlein, quoted earlier, suggested that our likelihood of getting into heaven is linked to the way we behave with cats. As we have, as a species, become much better at this, heaven must be a busy place.

Index

A
agreeableness 155

B
body clock 81
boxes 43–44

C
cat cafés 103
cat flaps 31
catnip 117
Cat Protection Society 54
chattering 28, 48, 159
children 7, 101, 130
claws 49
communication 96
constraints 159

D
dogs 5–6, 127–129
DNA 75

E
emotions 91, 94, 96
Erskineville, Cats of 54

F
feral 59
food 6, 16–17, 33–34
friendship 4, 20, 103, 125, 143

G
grooming 4

H
harness 159–161
hierarchy 99

H
Hooke's Law 147
humane societies 105, 108–109
humour 130

I
impulsiveness 154
indoor cats 115

K
kittens 5–6

L
laughing 162
law 5
leash 159

M
meow 93–95

N
neuroticism 150–151
neutering 60–61

P
politicians 104–106

R
rules 3

S
scratching 120
shelters 99, 100, 124
sleep 16, 43
smell 18, 43, 135
status 66

T
T.S. Eliot 2, 88
tigers 75–76

Photo credits

All photographs courtesy of Shutterstock, with the exception of the following:

Steve Bourne — pages 14, 16, 19

Isa Luerssen — pages 27, 42, 49, 129, 163

Alice Maxwell — pages 48, 64, 83, 165

Alyss Thomas — pages 8, 47, 71, 166

Endnotes

1. Litchfield, C.A., Quinton, G., Tindle, H., Chiera, B., Kikillus, K.H. and Roetman, P., 2017, 'The "Feline Five": An exploration of personality in pet cats (*Felis catus*)', PLoS One, vol. 12, no. 8, article no. e0183455, pp. 1–17.

2. https://www.sciencealert.com/ scientists-say-your-cat-is-probably-mirroring-your-own-personality